I0186882

SCOUT-SNIPING

BY

"PERISCOPE"

The Naval & Military Press Ltd

Published by

The Naval & Military Press Ltd

Unit 5 Riverside, Brambleside
Bellbrook Industrial Estate
Uckfield, East Sussex
TN22 1QQ England

Tel: +44 (0)1825 749494

www.naval-military-press.com
www.nmarchive.com

In reprinting in facsimile from the original, any imperfections are inevitably reproduced and the quality may fall short of modern type and cartographic standards.

PREFACE

THESE pages have been written in the hope of helping
Scout-Snipers of all ranks to discharge to the best
advantage the important duties for which they have
been selected.

Scout-Sniping is, beside being highly important,
also one of the most interesting branches of the Service.
On this branch rests the responsibility of obtaining
and forwarding information of everything done or
attempted by the enemy in No Man's Land, whilst
on the skill of the Scout-Snipers depend, not only
the safety of their own comrades, but also the gaining
for their side superiority of fire, by compelling the
enemy to keep close under cover, with a consequent
lowering of moral.

It is impossible to exaggerate the importance of
good Sniping and Scouting. When the Division,
Brigade, or Battalion is in the trenches, if the Sniping
Scout is good—

1. Many casualties will be avoided, because the
enemy Snipers will be reduced to impotence by being
unable to work without excessive risk of discovery
and death.

2. The moral of the enemy troops will be lowered,
and that of our own men correspondingly raised.

3. The danger of surprise is reduced to the lowest
possible point, as the enemy will be disinclined to
undertake minor offensive operations against us.

No effort is too great to ensure a pronounced superiority over the enemy in this respect.

Therefore, in the following pages, we will try and outline as clearly as possible the routine and nature of the training needed to raise Sniper Scouts to the necessary high standard. Our remarks and observations originated on Active Service, and though conditions change at different times on different parts of the line, our aim is to aid, if possible, Instructors and men to reach the very highest standard of efficiency.   We wish particularly to point out that of all the various specialists that this war has developed, the Sniper Scouts in connection with the Intelligence Branch are by far the most important, as their services are required every minute both day and night, and under all conditions of warfare.   They are the eyes and ears of the Army.

CONTENTS

LIST OF ILLUSTRATIONS

SCOUT-SNIPING

DUTIES OF A SCOUT-SNIPER.

SNIPING has now become a recognized factor in modern warfare. In August, 1914, when the enemy, full of hope, sure of victory, ordered her men to the conquest of Europe, she little thought that her enemies would have time to organize their resources to their advantage in time to save the situation ; so when the important branches of the Service were called out, naturally Sniping came well to the fore. It was in due time organized. For this work it is absolutely necessary to have the right man. A Sniper is not like a Bomber, whom you can train in the use of the several explosives, and, figuratively speaking, as long as he has an arm he will prove satisfactory. A Sniper needs more personal qualifications for results ; the arm of the Bomber corresponds to the brain of the Sniper. He must think, be able to observe, make use of cover, be able to shoot well, be capable, adaptable, and original. The N.C.O. in charge should be a strict disciplinarian, for in the carrying out of a Sniper's duties it is often necessary to relax discipline ; and unless the strictest measures are taken at home, you will find failure abroad due to the lack of active support from the men.

No one but the man· best adapted for this kind of work should be employed. A Sniper must be a past-master at shooting—not necessarily the School of Musketry as we know it. We should prefer the expert big-game hunter to the Bisley man, but a combination of both would be the best man that could be got. When a man is about to become a Sniper it is too late to begin to learn to shoot. He must already be an

B

expert shot. What he wants to think about is how to keep alive while discharging his duties, which is done by knowing how to take advantage of all natural, and construction of artificial, cover. A man's qualifications must be as follows :—

1. Must be sober and of temperate habits.

2. Must be physically fit for great strain and hardships.

3. Must be an accurate shot, deliberate and quick.

4. Must know how to do the right thing at the right time, and to do it quickly.

5. Must be a keen observer ; must be able to see without being seen.

6. Must know how to stalk without being seen or heard.

7. Must have and cultivate great patience.

8. Must be a good judge of distance.

9. Must have keen eyesight and good hearing.

10. Must know how to use telescope, periscope, hyposcope, sniperscope, magnifying sights, and telescopic rifle.

11. Must know how to take advantage of natural cover, and how to construct artificial cover.

12. Must understand the use of the compass, Prismatic Mark VII, oil, and plane.

13. Must be able to read a map.

14. Must have great self-control.

15. Must have strong will-power and determination.

16. Must be able to write short and concise reports.

17. Must be able to sketch.

18. Must know how to make and how to use decoys.

19. Must know how to locate enemy Snipers, Machine Guns, and Artillery by flash, sound, and bullet strike.

20. Must be a man who is a sticker.

21. Must be a man with courage combined with coolness.

22. Must be a man who is not slovenly, fussy, or one who panics.

23. Must understand the making and operating of rifle batteries.

24. Must understand Bombing.

25. Must know at least how to load, fire, and put out of action machine-guns.

26. Must understand gas protection.

NOTE.—If a man is good at night work, keep him as a night Scout; usually, as a rule, country-bred men are better than city-bred men. The men from the city learn very quickly, but from a Scouting point of view a man born among natural features is usually the best.

The duty of constant observation by day is very trying, but very interesting; a man must be carefully guarded *re* faking reports when, to use the slang expression, he is " fed up." This has been noted on the Western Front more than once, which resulted in the unnecessary loss of many men's lives.

Intelligent men with good education are usually the best, but this is not always possible.

You will find that, unless you get full co-operation from the Commanding Officer, it will be a very hard job to perfect these men to the necessary high standard. Early in the war Commanding Officers did not encourage this branch until they took their units to France and saw the extreme importance of it, the result being too late to train these men, and, again, unnecessary loss of life due to not sufficient information being gained.

Any man with the above qualifications will make a good Sniper Scout, and will be of great value to the Intelligence Department of the unit to which he belongs. A good Sniper is in most cases a good Scout; a good Scout is not always a Sniper, in many cases not being a good enough shot; but they should in their particular units work hand in hand, and be well versed in each other's doings for the benefit of the battalion to which they belong, and the cause in general.

Sniping is extremely interesting work, to match yourself against a cunning and experienced enemy, and be top dog, and stay that way. Take all the advantages you can get ; give none. If by any chance the enemy Sniper sees you, get him first ; to be too slow to shoot is dangerous, besides being a waste of time. A good Sniper Scout will always be thinking about his work, dream about it at night, invent all kinds of decoys and contrivances to conform with the local conditions.

The notes to be set forth will not cover all conditions ; besides, no one knows everything, though they ·may think they do. There are hundreds of big and little things about this work yet to be found out, invented, and to be put into actual use before this great war is over. Keep your mind busy on your work, and in connection with your daily practical experiences ; you might in many cases be benefited tomorrow by your experiences of to-day. Always bear in mind that when you are trying to locate the enemy Snipers, he is at the same time trying to locate you. An Officer should at no time carry a rifle when it interferes with his other duties. Snipers belonging to the same unit should constantly discuss ways and means amongst themselves—two heads are better than one—but they should never discuss these matters with strangers, not knowing whom they may be. If you have some ideas that will benefit other battalions, it will be communicated to them through the proper channels.

Your duty will be to worry the enemy night and day, give him no peace at any time. The least part of a man showing himself by day should be fired at, unless by waiting a little he will expose himself more, giving you a better chance to put him permanently out of action ; but this does not mean uselessly blazing away, which, of course, tends to give away your post or position.

There should be forty Scout-Snipers for a battalion. Now, in some battalions there may be ten, twelve, sixteen or more suitable men in one company, and none in the other. Train as a battalion, and transfer the certified men to the several companies, so that no one company will suffer from lack of efficiency in this branch. Nothing but the highest efficiency in shooting and trench craft should be considered in the appointment of a Sniper. Men should also, under the above-mentioned circumstances, be exchanged from one battalion to another in the same brigade, if by so doing higher efficiency could be reached ; and it is not fair to the Sniper Scout, after having arranged Sniping Posts, to return in your next tour of the trench and find that your post has been given away, due to the lack of efficiency in the relieved battalions. You must aim to improve conditions in the trenches that you take over, both as to safety and comfort, and take pride in leaving something behind you that will puzzle your successor to improve upon. In making improvements on advanced Sniping Posts in particular, great care must be taken that, in so doing, you don't overdo anything, and thereby give your position away. The old saying that " What was good enough for my father is good enough for me " is a curse in modern warfare. We live in an age of progress. We are either going to be the best or the enemy is : don't let him be. Take advantage of everything at your disposal, with an eye to improvement. Explain thoroughly to the Sniper that relieves you, after showing him all the ins and outs of your improvements, your reasons for the same. We have no trade secrets or patents, except as far as the enemy are concerned. Any idea you may have let your brother Sniper benefit by it. Nothing but our united efforts will lead to success.

Qualifications of Snipers are of two classes—NATURAL and ACQUIRED. A Marksman is born, not made. All the training in the world cannot make a Marksman of everybody. You can by persistent practice make a good shot of almost anybody, but you cannot make a Marksman of everybody. None but the best should satisfy you in this line ; we are rather limited for men at our disposal. Even when you are a natural-born Marksman, it takes a great deal of constant practice to attain the highest efficiency, and also a lot of practice to hold your position once that you have got it. That being the case, a Sniper should fire a few shots each day at prominent objects where he or his observer can see the bullet strike, and also for the purpose of obtaining exact ranges at the enemy's parapet, or other places where he is likely to expose himself. You should not, however, shoot at the exact spot that you expect someone to expose himself, but a spot close by at the same range. It is of the greatest help to the Sniper if he has been a big-game hunter; if he is a target shot only, you will find that he dwells too long on his aim. He must overcome this by practising quick aiming and trigger-pressing. The first aim is always the clearest. If you aim a long time your eyes get blurred, and your nerves give way, and, worst of all, the enemy might get you first if you happen to be exposed to his aim. Any Sniper who finds himself in this position should practise at disappearing targets, with shorter exposures as he gains in efficiency. Unless a man has already qualified as far as shooting is concerned, he must not be taken on as a Sniper.

As you will see by qualifications, a man must be of sober and temperate habits; he must never drink or smoke while occupying a Sniping Post, as drink dulls and shakes his nerves, and smoking gives his position away. He must be in the best of health; his eyesight must be perfect, or he cannot qualify. Some of the most excellent shots use eye-glasses. It would in many cases be dangerous in this game, as the sun might be at an angle, and heliograph your position to the enemy.

ORGANIZATION OF SNIPERS AND SCOUTS.

A specially appointed Officer in the Army Corps Staff should have control of organization, employment, and disposition of all Snipers in the Corps, also one Divisional, one Brigade, and one Battalion Sniping Officer. This is being successfully done now by the Intelligence Officer.

Snipers must form a separate unit in the battalion, and should live apart from their companies, should never be employed in any ordinary work, and should wear a special badge ; the Officer in Charge to see that they are kept to the standard with regard to discipline. A Sniper is a specialist, but only when he is so employed. He must not forget that he must at all times be amenable to military discipline.

The strength of Snipers in the battalion should be as follows :—

1 Officer.
8 N.C.Os.
32 men.

No preference as to who should be a Sniper must in any case be given ; nothing but qualifications must be considered. Any man selected for a Sniper must at least be a first-class shot. The same qualifications must apply to the Officer and N.C.Os., as it would be a crime to put such highly-trained men under anyone who is superior to them in rank only. The best man is the volunteer.

If Snipers are employed before regular Sniping organization has been adopted in the battalion, they should be left to their own resources, given liberty of action, live with their company, report daily to the Company Officer through the proper channel, but should be exempt from all other duties. They should work in pairs or threes. In regard to discipline, pay, and rations, they will form part of their company. None but fully-qualified Snipers should be employed in this way.

There should be two posts on each company frontage, with three men manning each, and two spare men will have a roving commission along their company frontage, under the O.C. Scout-Sniper's directions ; they will make, place, and manipulate decoys, and prepare rifle batteries for night firing, etc.

When posts are accessible in the daytime, reliefs should take place every two hours. This is done by

the rovers or the support company Snipers, and only
one man should be relieved at one time from each post.
That will relieve each individual every four hours.
O.C. Snipers must see that they are always on the
alert. This is an all-the-time job ; every minute
counts. A Sniper falling asleep or otherwise neglect-
ing his duties should be severely punished.

A detached advanced post where no communication
can be maintained in the daytime should have a 'phone
or signal wire, so O.C. Snipers can readily obtain information. The senior N.C.O. or Sniper in command
of post will be the one responsible for writing the daily
report, and will be held responsible for general conduct
and efficiency of that particular post.

. Any casualties must be included in the daily report,
with full explanations and details. Any Sniper
putting in a wrong or exaggerated report should be
severely dealt with.

It may, under special certain conditions, be necessary
to have more or less than six fixed Sniping Posts in connection with the three companies occupying the front
line of trenches. In that case some or all of the support company Snipers may be used. It would be well
to have several spare Sniping Posts under ordinary conditions. You then could move about, and not be shooting continuously from the same place, and on special
occasions the spare posts would be useful for the support Snipers. Then in other cases good work might
be done from the support trenches. The two men
who are Rovers to-day will each relieve a man in the
fixed Sniping Post to-morrow. That means that each
Sniping Post is always manned by one man that was
there the day before. This being the case, the battalion that relieves you must send in one man for each
Sniping Post the day before the battalion takes over
the trenches. These advance Snipers report to, and
come under the direction of, the present O.C. Snipers,
but make their daily reports to their own O.C. Snipers
when he takes over the next night. O.C. Snipers must

make himself perfectly familiar with each Sniping Post under his command. He must also know the individual ability of men under his command, and employ them accordingly. Some men shoot quicker than others ; such men are best employed on the shorter range, where the enemy show themselves for a very short period. Then there is the specialist in long-range work. PUT THE RIGHT MAN IN THE RIGHT PLACE.

A diary must be kept of every Sniping Post by O.C. Snipers, and should consist of all the Snipers' daily reports. The O.C. Snipers must give a receipt in writing when taking over relieved battalion's diary, and *vice versa*. All O.C. Snipers must keep a copy of diary, and have one sent to Battalion and Brigade Headquarters. This diary must be at all times accessible to the Intelligence Department, also to the artillery observer ; but no one must at any time read the same, or any part thereof, without properly establishing their identity. Anyone allowing anyone to be in possession of or read any part of a Sniper's diary should be severely dealt with.

If these rules are strictly observed, it will be of great value in many ways. Sniper Scouts should also receive any information procured by airmen, artillery observer, etc., that will be of any value to them. Co-OPERATION IS VERY ESSENTIAL.

EQUIPMENT.

It does not matter how efficient a Scout-Sniper may be, if he has nothing to work with, or insufficient equipment, both as to quality and to quantity, he is severely handicapped. This branch of the Service is of sufficient importance to warrant the best of everything ; we demand the highest possible qualifications in the man selected for this work, and it is but fair to him that we should give him the best equipment obtainable.

If using the Ross pattern, or the new 1914 Lee-Enfield rifles, and you have to shoot at night, fill the sight-protecting hood over your foresight full of white wood or paper, raise your backsight up as far as it will go (with the screw), use the square opening thus produced for your rear aperture sight, the result being a fairly accurate shot. This will be especially useful for Scouts at night, or Snipers encountering enemy patrols on leaving advanced posts. That is, when it is too dark to shoot in the usual way.

After 2,000 shots a Sniper should have a new rifle. A rifle that has been condemned by a Sniper might still be of use to the infantry. Never pick a rifle with a bright yellow butt or forearm, nor a very dark one. The barrel should be painted grey. The bright muzzle of a new rifle might give your position away if not painted. Under many circumstances green would be a better colour. It will also in many cases be of advantage to have the whole rifle painted, telescopic sight and all, if one is used. If you are issued with a telescopic rifle, it will be properly cleaned and returned to O.C. Snipers at night, with your other special equipment, and reissued in the morning. Each Sniping Post should have at least one telescopic rifle. If enough could be got, each Sniper should have his own, as it will not work out satisfactory in practice to allow several Snipers to use the same telescopic rifle. The O.C. Snipers must understand how to adjust all kinds of telescopic sights, although some of the sights must not be touched apart from the focussing, but are to be sent back to the makers for readjustment. Any telescopic sight is easily put out of order, and if you are allowed to adjust them and you do not know how, the sight is useless.

We recommend the use of a ·440 high-velocity rifle for smashing loophole plates.

A telescope or a pair of field-glasses is needed per post. A very powerful telescope is better for this work than field-glasses, for your loophole is usually too small for the glasses unless it is a single binocular. Also, by having a compass, a Sniper can send in a more intelligent report.

There should be at least one periscope to each Sniping Post, and the Rovers should have one each. In advanced or other concealed Sniping Posts a periscope will not be necessary. They are used chiefly when operating from the trenches.

All rifles that have been damaged beyond repair should be used for dummy Sniping Posts, with or without the dummy sniper, to draw the enemy fire. Snipers' coats, long, green, or other colours to conform to the surroundings, should be supplied by the Brigade. These coats will be found very useful to assimilate the surroundings. Also veil or mask to suit, and covering for the hands of the same material. It is wonderful what stalking an expert can do when assimilated to the surroundings, and also be able to occupy an advanced and exposed post without fear of detection. A grass head-cover is very useful when well made. Other material to be indented for by O.C. Snipers is as follows :—Ropes for climbing trees (with big trunks) for placing snipers or decoys. Wires of different gauge to manipulate decoys. Paint-brushes and ready-mixed paint of colours to suit requirements for rifles, etc. Steel plates for making loopholes. Sandbags for constructing special Sniping Posts. A few yards of factory cotton for making faces for decoys. Needles and strong thread. Wire netting, lumber and timber for constructing posts, old clothing, caps, and boots, for dressing decoys.

You will want also prismatic compass, wire cutters, a revolver for night scouting, and a few Véry light pistols to be attached to section.

DAY WORK.

There is a great deal to do for a Scout-Sniper by day, as you will see later. The kind of work he does varies. With Snipers these days the total number of the enemy killed is not the great thing, though very important. It is upon the Scout-Sniper that the Brigade relies for information and reports. The information is asked for, and it is up to you to find the means by which it can be obtained.

There are various posts and plans from which information can be found. Posts are divided into three kinds :—

1. Organized or Fixed.
2. Unorganized, but Fixed.
3. Moving or Rovers' Posts.

An Organized Post is a post dug in, whether in No Man's Land in the parapet, in the parados, in the reserves, or anywhere which is permanent. This post is used by Snipers daily.

The Unorganized but the Fixed Post might be well dug in, but used at various times, not continually. Of course, this keeps the enemy guessing as to your whereabouts. If you spotted an enemy's Unorganized Post in No Man's Land, what would you do ? The enemy will do the same.

The moving Sniper, known as the Rover, wanders around the trenches, hedges, shell-holes, and old buildings, etc., and takes the pot shot. There has been great argument as to using buildings as posts, but we will not commit ourselves ; for there were buildings on the front which we could use with comparative safety, and there were others which it would be suicide to go near. This is where the common sense of the individual Sniper comes in ; but if you are using a building for a Fixed Post, do not hesitate to sandbag it well in. We will explain the construction of Sniping Posts later. Having manned a post, we say to ourselves, What instruments are necessary to man this ? The answer to that is : Telescope rifle, periscope, field-glasses or telescope, and perhaps a dagger-knife, a knife of this kind being a silent and useful weapon for night work. These posts should be manned by two or three men, not more, as constant observation is very trying. Allow one man to observe for twenty minutes, one man to shoot, and one to act as runner, the runner being responsible for messages back to

Headquarters. If your post is in No Man's Land and your report cannot be taken back, he must devise some original means by which they can be. That is his responsibility. Your post must be continually in touch with the F.O.O. (artillery), Machine-Gunners, Trench Mortars, Bombers, and Front Line Trench.

From your post a detailed range card and sketch should be made, upon which must be described all minute details on your sector, such as shell-holes, upturned sods, craters, old tins, sandbags, etc. ; anything noticed must be constantly watched and continually observed, and reported back.

The posts, sector or frontage, will not be over a hundred yards, so this can easily be done ; by doing this, and continuous study of No Man's Land, any change will be readily noted, and naturally suspicion will be aroused.

Remember, persistently hammering at one spot tells tremendously, but remember that watching is much more important than uselessly blazing away.

After concealing yourself—that is, in your post or in the roving position that you are sniping from—you must conceal your fire from the Sniper's point of view. This is quite easy to understand, for the flash of a single shot might give away a post which took weeks to construct. If the country is construed with gorse, the same can be put in front of your loophole and shot through, thus hiding the flash. The cover in front of the loophole would correspond with the surrounding natural features. Hold your rifle 2 feet in rear of opening. Remember, you want front, rear, and overhead cover, and you want to fire at an angle ; not only will your loophole be less likely spotted, but your flash less likely seen. Have the background inside your post correspond with that in the front. It is far easier to see through a loophole with a white background than one with a dark one. In all cases beware of the silhouette effect.

Each and every man must have patience ; it is a great thing. As you control your cycle or your motor-car, so must you control your actions. If it is necessary to take ten minutes to fire a shot, take it, and don't forget to always have a reason for shooting, such as unnatural movement of bush, etc. If you fire at anything where you expect someone to be, but are not quite sure, never fire a single shot only, but fire several shots at the same place ; if an enemy Sniper is actually there, you may kill him, but if you don't hit him, you may make him think that you have definitely located him, and he won't fire from there any more. In this connection, always bear in mind that all unnecessary shooting should be avoided, as it may give your position away. BE SUSPICIOUS ; ONCE SUSPICIOUS, YOU WATCH ; ONCE YOU WATCH, YOU LEARN.

As to the kind of information wanted about the enemy in your own sector : Loopholes in any part of their trenches or otherwise ; unnatural movements ; Sniping Posts in trees, hedges, farmhouses, craters, shell-holes, etc. ; information about his stores, trenches, wires, activity, dumping ground, gaps in parapet ; points from where he can best be sniped ; fires where cooking goes on ; fixed rifles, machine-guns, bombing points, saps, uniforms, habits, etc. ; reports on aeroplanes or aircraft of any kind ; direction from and where going (remember that time is imperative) ; enemy's guns (calibre), and, roughly, direction. Wind is most important in these barbarous times, and the slightest change must be noted and reported at once. Now, these are some of the things to be noted, but there are more ; something new arises daily, so watch hard, and, as we have said before, patiently.

Information about our own lines is important ; you ask yourself why ? If you have your post in No Man's Land, can't you see our lines as the enemy sees it ? Then report fully in what places improvements can be made. Suggest new points for observation and

Sniping. Report the dangerous places in our line where the enemy snipe, and give the direction of same. If it is out of your sector, pass the information on to the post responsible ; if not, it is up to you to deal with him. Report anything that will be of use in the perfecting of your own front ; it is marvellous the good such information as this does.

Man your post with the same men until they thoroughly know their frontage ; each inch wants to be known like the ABC's. Knowing that, let them move to the immediate right or left, and so on, until they thoroughly know their whole battalion frontage.

It is important that you should train your eyesight, not only the naked eye, but with glasses and telescope, now before going abroad. A little time each day should be spent, for the more you look at one spot the more you see. All movement is suspicious—a branch apparently blown by the wind, the flight of birds, etc. —so watch every movement hard. Your sector should be under constant observation every minute of daylight. At first you may think you may have seen everything ; don't fool yourself, there is something new to see every day.

A Sniping Post should be manned before dawn, and not quitted until after dark. It is of little use to tell you that once your post is discovered by the enemy, it is of little use to you, so don't fire too often, or it will disclose your position. This is where patience is taxed. Don't be in a hurry to fire ; make sure of your target first, figure on 50—50, and if you are a good shot you will seldom lose. A good plan is not to fire for some time ; that will entice the enemy to come out ; he will get careless, then the odds are yours.

Build dummy loopholes, not too many, in your trenches ; have them marked, and let the enemy play with them. It will keep them guessing whether they are manned or not, and, as will be explained later, will give you a chance to locate enemy positions. Give them a few shots from it now and then to encourage them along a bit. Always remember that though you are trying to get the enemy, he is at the same time trying to get you.

In ordinary every-day trench warfare we think that nobody but the Snipers should fire ; of course, if there was an attack or daylight raid, matters would alter, but otherwise it would be a saving of ammunition with about the same results. All advanced Sniping Posts should be manned and guarded at night, and can nearly always be used with advantage as listening posts. It is dangerous to leave them unoccupied, as the enemy might find them and mine them, or have the other branches, such as machine-guns, trench mortars, artillery, etc., surprise you in the morning.

Co-operate with the F.O.O. (artillery) ; learn what he knows ; also with the Air Service, and obtain the use of photographs from aeroplanes. These will aid your findings wonderfully well. Any information received should be immediately signalled to you.

NIGHT WORK.

Let us divide night work into two parts :—(1) Night Sniping and Observation from Posts ; (2) Patrol Work.

If you believed that you could snipe the enemy by night by the help of star-shells, either their defects in parapet or working parties, then, of course, you would do so ; but remember, if you have a good post in No Man's Land, do not foolishly give it away by attempting night work, for the flash of a rifle is much easier seen by night than it is by day. If you are so well concealed that the flash cannot be seen, then, of course, it would be all right.

At night is the time for the roving Sniper ; he can crawl out to shell-holes, depressions, mine-craters, etc., and spend a jolly evening playing with the enemy working parties.

Before going out on patrol for information there are many things that you want to think about. Nothing is so foolish as to go aimlessly over the para-

PREPARATION FOR TRAINING IN THE USE OF DISGUISES IN SYMPATHY WITH THE NATURAL FEATURES OF LANDSCAPE.

MEN PREPARING THEMSELVES FOR STALKING UNDER VARIOUS CONDITIONS.

USE OF COVER.
These men were six yards apart before seeing each other.

SHOWING THE REFLECTION OF THE SUN ON THE RIFLE, AND HOW THE WIRED SERVICE CAP SHOWS UP.

pet. In different sectors you have different depths
of No Man's Land. Even in battalion frontage it
often varies, and sometimes considerably. Supposing
you were ordered to obtain certain information from
a certain sector *re* the enemy's wire, its condition,
depth, etc., whether it has been cut or not. Your
patrol would consist of about three, no more ; it is
information you want, and this number is plenty.
What would you first think of ? It is dangerous to
go out without warning your sentries from what point
you are going out, and time that you are returning ;
rightly would they shoot you if you did not. Then
think of the ground that you are going to cover ; you
have been studying it by day by periscope or through
loophole, and know every detail ; you have pictured
the places you are going over the parapet (and if
caught by star-shell slowly close eyes), the position
where you are going through your own wires, and how
you are going to get across No Man's Land ; the lay
of the land, the disposition of your men in crawling,
etc.

In ninety-nine cases out of a hundred you will be
successful ; but supposing one of your men knocks a
tin or rings a bell attached to a wire, the result would
be continuous star-shells. Then lie still and flat, face
and hands covered. If caught standing and the star-
shell bursts, remain perfectly rigid, and lower head,
and place hands slowly behind back ; if you are seen
then, and you know the position of a shell-hole, get to
it as quickly as possible.

While on patrol duty never hurry ; crawl slowly
and quietly, heels well down, face and hands covered
with paint or mud. The skin is what shows up. For
every look in front give ten behind ; of course, this is
exaggerated, but it is to impress on you the extreme
importance of doing the same. When looking back,
do not raise your head above your right or left shoulder,
but raise your right or left upper arm on a level with
the shoulder, and look back under the armpit ; by this

c

means nothing will protrude higher than the original thickness of the body. When in No Man's Land, look back and spot all land-marks, and mark them in relation to the point where you came out of the trench ; if it is too dark to do that, feel the condition of the earth at that point—it might tell you something ; or put a notch in the entanglement piquet, and remember the number of yards left or right of that. If you don't do these things, you will find yourself in No Man's Land one day with dawn breaking, and it will be necessary for you to crawl into a shell-hole and spend the day. Never move more than ten yards without lying perfectly still and listening for at least two minutes ; by doing this, you know if an enemy patrol is out, or you can hear enemy wiring parties, if any, location of, etc. Nevertheless, if you are out after information, get it ; that's your duty. It is far better than combat, for if in an encounter you are made a casualty, the information will be lost or delayed. At all hazards, mark the entrance and re-entrance of your own and enemy's wire. Now, in England, is the time to train your men to cut wire correctly. Inexperienced men have gone out on patrol, incorrectly cut the wire ; it has sprung, with the result that the patrol was given away, and the night's work a failure. Never let this be said of your patrol.

In returning to your own lines with information, there is a tendency in men to make a bolt for it. Do not allow such a thing. It is a dangerous practice, and, if killed, likely the information will never be received. Be as precautious coming in as you were going out. This is important.

Upon returning to your trench each write a report on your night's work. Never under any circumstances talk about what you have seen to each other until you have each written a clear report on what you think you saw. It is so easy for a man to change his ideas on information received from another ; this is a great mistake, for the other might not be right ; the result would be disaster, and perhaps the unnecessary loss of many men's lives.

Remember, when crawling, that after you have gone about ten yards, and you stop to listen, you hear an enemy patrol on your right ; the nearer you get to them, and they find you, the less chance they have of bombing you, for the effect of the bomb would be as disastrous to them as it would be to you.

It is not wise when on information patrols to take any equipment whatever, not even a rifle ; a hand-axe or bayonet is useful and silent, and a couple of Mills in each pocket as a last resource. A rifle is cumbersome ; it is information you want, and not an engagement with the enemy. A properly trained Sniper Scout is safer than the ordinary rifleman in the trench.

If your moral is good, it will be only a few patrols before you are trying various schemes on the enemy, and confidence of moving in No Man's Land, though under different conditions, as you would across Piccadilly Circus. If on any rough ground you trip or kick something which causes an unnecessary noise, lay perfectly still ; it is the only way to escape observation, and by so doing it keeps the enemy in doubt as to your numbers, intentions, etc.

USE OF SCOUT-SNIPER UNDER VARIOUS CONDITIONS.

Your men must be thoroughly trained for all contingencies. You never know at what time the forces in the field will break into open warfare, so naturally when they do the scouting ability of your men will come well to the fore. Here is where observation, stalking, use of cover, etc., is essential. Supposing the troops now were in open warfare, what would be the use of the Sniper Scout ?

Now, let us take troops at the halt first. You know by your infantry training that when a body of troops are halted, there must be a body of troops detailed to protect them ; therefore a piquet line or line of

c 2

resistance is planned and manned ; from this line sentry groups are put out, and ahead of these groups your work comes in. You will patrol the country in pairs at the distance of one to two miles in depth—more, if necessary—and ascertain any information that will be of any use to the piquet line. You must let your piquet line and your sentry groups know that you are out, or trouble will ensue, the same as a patrol from a trench. It is important that all roads be carefully watched, and that no enemy Scouts see you, so practise the use of cover at home before going abroad. It is essential and necessary at all times.

From this we continue to troops on the move. Picture to yourself a battalion or brigade moving up a road. The protective force here consists of the advance guard, consisting of the main and vanguards. Ahead of these move the Scouts ; their business is to search everything that might hide the enemy *en route*, for machine-guns, artillery, infantry, or otherwise ; houses, strawstacks, trees, and everything must be thoroughly searched. Even if the houses, strawstacks, etc., do look deserted, fail not in your duty by not searching ; never commit yourself to such a blunder. A case happened in France whereby a battalion was on the move ; this was in the earlier part of the war. The Scouts passed an old house which was about twenty yards back from the right of the road ; to all appearance, it was deserted : the blinds were drawn, there was no smoke from the chimney, and it looked desolate. They sent back no report, not having searched it, the result being that the cyclists and the advance guards were allowed to pass, and when the main body came up machine-guns played havoc with them through the dominating windows and blinds. It was too late to remedy the mistake ; the carelessness of a few caused the lives of many to be lost. Now, these things will happen until men are chosen who can use their brains. It is up to your Commanding Officer to allow you the best men to train, and the Officer is responsible for training them thoroughly. Never lose track of the body that you are screening; this might prove disastrous, for if you lose time in finding them, likely by the time you do the Commander will not have time to deploy before the enemy is upon him.

Scouts will be necessary for the flanks, as well as in advance of the advance guard. You never know at what time the enemy will surprise you by moving around your flank and cutting you off in the rear.

I draw your attention to the use of Scouts when troops are in extended order, when about to engage the enemy. They should be well pushed out with relays back to the front line, in order that any message may be got back quickly, without allowing the Scout to leave his position for any length of time. The first Scout, after returning to No. 1 relay with his message, can return immediately to his position and carry on with his observations, while No. 2 relay takes it back to No. 3, and so on.

Let us take the same men being used as Snipers in the advance guard. They would work with the vanguard, and use their intelligence as to action as much as possible. If coming in touch with the enemy, those who are not on Scouting duty would push forward and take up high positions, and by accurate shooting would worry the enemy while the Commander is making plans of attack. In the advance from the trench the Sniper is exceedingly useful, and his work considerable. As a rule, the infantry are held up at about the third or fourth line; this is the time the Sniper should be under the direct control of the Sniping Officer, who brings them up with the support, and puts them on the track of the machine-guns which are holding back our infantry. They can be the cause of many casualties amongst the panic-stricken retreaters also.

The part played by the Sniper in the rear-guard is also of extreme importance. The object of a rear-guard is to delay the enemy, and, if possible, make him deploy, so as to allow one's main force to gain a place of safety. With this object in view the guarding force wants to be as small as possible. These are stretched out to make the enemy believe that there are greater numbers. Now the intelligence, quick wit, and originality of the Sniper tell. The game is to make each shot tell ; the more casualties you inflict, the lower their moral becomes, and time is wasted. There are many things a Sniper can do in a rear-guard if he will only use his brains, and properly trained men, you will find, will not fail you.

The above are various uses, apart from trench warfare, of the Scout-Sniper. What these men should know will be explained in the following pages. Each and every Scout-Sniper should be trained alike in order that one is capable of doing the work of the other.

SNIPERS IN ATTACK AND DEFENCE.

If an attack is to be made, it will be well to have additional Sniping Posts if advanced posts are used, so that the Rovers can be on the spot, and, if possible, make posts for the Snipers belonging to the support company. You can cover the advance of the troops in the rear by quick and accurate fire, and, as likely as not, as before stated, put the enemy's machine-guns out of action. If the enemy does not know from whence the fire comes, serious damage can be inflicted. If there is a depression in front of you, and your troops advance, you can stay where you are giving protective fire, in case the enemy wire is to be cut. You must under no consideration get out of your advanced post when under observation by the enemy. Only when our men are entering the enemy's trenches do you make haste and move forward, and take up better positions, so that your infantry will further benefit by your marksmanship. You at once begin to take notice as to location of new Sniping Posts, in or in front of the new position, and have them constructed and occupied at once.

In a general advance the O.C. Snipers should see that the whole unit benefits by your marksmanship, by properly distributing Snipers along the unit's front ; but each Sniper should not be tied down to hard-and-fast rules in the firing line, but allowed to use his own judgment as to the position which would be of the most use to him and to those he is protecting. Snipers should never take part as an average rifleman in a night attack, for his marksmanship is of no value, but should be on hand to take every advantage of the result of the attack, choose his best positions and man it before dawn; keep cool. If you can get a good elevated position close up to the enemy's lines, and well concealed, you can make it very warm for their reinforcements. The enemy's bombers may also require some attending to. Don't use a position too far back, for then you will come under the enemy's artillery fire. You must keep a sharp look-out for the enemy Sniper ; likely he will be doing the same thing, so put him out of action before he can do you any harm, or the men which you are screening. If you find that in the advance it is necessary to shoot over the heads of your own men, be very careful that you do not shoot directly over a man, for he might rise at any time. When you are in front of your own men, you want to be well bullet-proof concealed from the rear, because they are not as expert marksmen as yourself. In the advance any Sniper's equipment in the possession of the individual Snipers—that is, apart from what he needs—must be left safely behind, and the O.C. Snipers must make arrangements to have this reserve collected and guarded, and reissued later when convenient. When in the firing line with other troops, give them the benefit of your superior knowledge as to range. At any time when you find any wounded, fix his bayonet in his rifle, and shove the bayonet down in the ground, so that a stretcher-bearer can easily find him. You may save a man's life this way, and very much facilitate the work of the search-parties and stretcher-bearers. In case the attack should fail, concealed as Snipers on each company front, you would be invaluable in covering the retreat of your unit across No Man's Land back to your own trenches, doing a great deal of harm to the enemy. You will remain in your post until dark, as usual, until relieved by the night guard or listening post.

In the case of the enemy's surprise attack, pick off their men until they are close to you, then lay still and let them pass. If your post is concealed as it ought to be, your post won't be discovered. It is as well to have three or four extra rations, for if their attack is successful, you will now be in the rear of their lines. If unfortunate enough to become a prisoner, play the fool and say nothing ; destroy your equipment or any military information. If not found out, you may do useful work for two or three days behind their lines, as they have done behind ours ; but, if possible, crawl through their lines and back at night ; this has often been done. You have confidence, anyway, that your troops will counter-attack, so stick and remain cool as long as possible, or as long as you may think it advisable for your own benefit and the cause in general. In a case of this kind it is not so hard to get back to your own lines as it may appear on the surface. Penetrating the enemy's lines from his rear is much easier than from his front. Take your time ; take advantage of everything to cover your movements—of any noises going on, talking of enemy's sentries, the moon disappearing behind clouds, etc. When the star-shells go up, close your eyes, as you can see better in the dark afterwards. When you approach your own lines, take cover in a shell-hole or any good cover before you challenge a sentry, and be sure it is your own sentry that you are dealing with.

When the enemy is preparing an attack, there is generally the usual preparatory bombardment of your trenches. This bombardment will not affect you if you are properly located—ahead of our trenches for preference, or in rear of them if necessity demands.

It all depends on local conditions. Now, if our own artillery is not shelling the enemy's trenches at the same time, they will consider themselves quite safe in looking over to see the effect of their shells on our trenches ; that is just what you are looking for. You can make a good bag in this way. If your Sniping Post is in your trenches when they are being bombarded, you can do no good there ; far better seek a place of safety, as you will be a valuable man to have when the bombardment is over and the enemy launches his attack. If you leave your post in the face of an enemy attack, you must in all cases blow it up. In some places local conditions will be such that you can retire without being exposed to the fire of either side, but if you have nerve and sufficient confidence in yourself, you will do more good by sticking in your post, provided it is properly concealed. An open top post would be hopeless. There is only one thing to do—retire—and in doing so take advantage of every available cover. You may also save yourself by having a tunnel to some other place (a few yards will do) that is more concealed, but not so good to shoot from as your regular post, having just loopholes and no exit. Now, if you are discovered, and the enemy call on you to surrender, and lots of them stand about, retire to your auxiliary post and blow up your main post, and some of the enemy may go with it. Now, they have every reason to think that you blew yourself up also, as part of connecting tunnel will have fallen in during the explosion. If you succeed at this, you can dig yourself out at leisure or when you think best. It is a poor fox that has but one hole, and of two evils choose the least. This, of course, applies to a concealed post. In the rear-guard action all Snipers should be in the extreme rear, with the machine-gunners told off for this purpose. The enemy's progress can be greatly impeded, if not entirely stopped. At any rate, you can hold them up until the troops in the rear have been able to take up an advantageous position. This work should be done under the personal supervision of the Battalion

O.C. Snipers. For observation holes from Sniping Posts or a fire trench at various angles you can often use a trench augur to advantage. It only takes a few minutes to bore through, and if results are not satisfactory, you can make another one.

Now, in advancing into enemy's country or country where you are likely to encounter enemy patrols, Scouts, etc., you proceed very cautiously, and see without being seen ; search all likely and unlikely cover as you advance, and take notice of any signs of any kind that are left behind by the enemy, and search the country well ahead of you, taking care to note the things on both your flanks, as you can often, by close observation, see objects a long way off to your right or left better than those Scouts on whose front it occurs. Glance back every little while, and picture what the country looks like behind you, so that you will be able to recognize natural features upon return. It will be rarely wise for Scouts to fire at anybody or anything ; but, being a highly-trained man and above the average intelligence, you should instantly consider the advantage and disadvantage resulting from such action. If a lot of firing is going on everywhere, and your own firing does not give your position away, you become a Sniper as well as a Scout for the moment ; so you see the difference between this kind of work and pure and simple Sniping. When employed only in the capacity of Sniping, you must always kill an enemy on sight ; when Scouting, you must do the same, but only when considering circumstances and possible consequences you find it wise to do so. In Scouting you will often have to beat a hasty retreat, so when passing over the country take notice of all cover in your rear, so you can return without being seen. If you meet the enemy Scouts, don't ever let them go back and report to their own lines.

The troops in your rear may have to open fire at any moment ; it would be a pity if you should afterwards hear : " Well, we did not succeed because we had to waste our best opportunity waiting for the Scouts to come in." It should be understood that the Scouts are quite capable of taking care of themselves ; so in this connection you always examine the ground as a matter of course. It should never be hard for you to find suitable cover on a second's notice. When the firing starts you must join in ; and if it is long-range work, the trajectory of the opposing firing lines will be in your favour, and you can do great damage to the enemy yourself at your comparatively close range, the enemy not knowing you are there. Being a good Scout, you are not very likely to be caught in this way in very close action. If so, you must use your own judgment ; keep cool, and, with your ability and education in Scouting and Sniping, you should come out all right. Always bear in mind that, whatever tactics you are using, the enemy may possibly practise the same ; don't let him be first.

INTELLIGENCE.

Every Scout-Sniper should be an Intelligence Department of his own. He must realize the vast importance of keeping everything quiet. It is a very serious offence for any man to let out any military information, but with a Sniper Scout it is worse than a mere offence ; it is a crime that should call for a very severe penalty. A Sniper Scout should know better ; there has been too much information leaking out of late ; wherever you go, you hear soldiers discussing this, that, and the other thing. It is wrong— entirely wrong. Everybody looks forward to the end of the war ; how do you ever expect it to end if you let out what you are going to do ? Men are careless when they are on leave, either from lack of something to say or because they are interested. It was just the other day that we were going up to a certain city, and an officer was home from the front on leave. We asked him a few questions as to the conditions at the front now. We got our reply all right, and more ;

he became so infused with some of our new instruments
that he told us all about them, even to the most minute
details. You see that this is a mistake, but you see
when it is too late. In mixing with women, perfect
strangers, often military information is confidentially
given. There are women who are the greatest spies
that the world has ever known ; they have their con-
temporaries, and you don't know who they are or where
they are. Remember, when it is military information,
be silent when strangers are about.

You know that in the last few years we have been
on the decline ; in a few more years likely we would
have been in the decayed stage. We are old-fashioned,
slow, bad observers. This country has but one to
thank for her regeneration, and that is the enemy,
who is showing us at the cost of her downfall. We
know of a case where a man knew of a German, and
suspected espionage, but was afraid of reporting it
for fear of making a fool of himself. Many men in
France are continually losing their lives in doing their
duty. Do you see the point ? Are you the careless
one ? There are many actual happenings in France
very interesting,·but very regrettable, which we would
like to tell you about, but time forbids. If you will
take the advice of one who feels for the lives of others,
remember when it is a matter of military importance
SAY NOTHING. Intelligence, if fully explained, would
be more than time or pages would allow. In the above
paragraphs we have tried to explain as far as possible
as it would affect the Sniper Scout. The main point
to be remembered is SILENCE, and if you carry out
your duty as Sniper Scouts your information will be
readily obtained and be of use. Let nothing escape
your notice, for everything that is done there is always
a reason. Keep your eyes and ears open, no matter
where you are. If you suspect anyone, do not let them
know it, as it will put them on their guard. The most
innocent-looking and acting of those people who are
out to obtain information are usually the most dan-

gerous, for your suspicion will not likely be aroused. You may be the cause of heavy losses to life and property by too much talking. No matter who may ask, when it is about military information say nothing. Obtain all the information you can, but give none. The enemy are constantly impressing upon their soldiers and sailors the value of silence pertaining to military matters.

In dealing with prisoners, study your man ; remember your business is to get all possible information out of him. There are different means in handling the prisoner in this respect ; you must either treat him with kindness or sympathy, or by treating him harshly. It all depends on the man, and in what circumstances he was taken. Don't take everything for granted what he tells you.

When a patrol or a party of the enemy approaches your line to surrender voluntarily, and call upon you to come out of your trenches and take them, don't go, as it is likely a trick that they are trying to play on you. In the daytime you may be sure that it is so, for if the enemy trenches were manned they would be shot down by their own men. Call for them one at a time, and search them immediately for concealed arms. If they refuse to come in or start to run back, shoot them. Never trust to their white flag. With regard to kindness to deserters, by acting intelligently in this respect desertion from the enemy's lines will be greatly encouraged, and a genuine deserter usually brings very valuable information ; but he will only come over when he thinks it safe to do so.

When in pursuit of the enemy, take the greatest of precautions, and be suspicious of everything ; take nothing for granted. An innocent helmet lying on the field may be a contrivance to kill by having a bomb fixed under it. Any other equipment might be similarly fixed. They have been known to place live bombs under dead bodies, which, when removed, exploded. Guard against any buildings or bridges left intact by the enemy ; likely they will be mined. Don't eat or drink anything the enemy have left behind before it has been thoroughly examined by competent authorities. Watch carefully the attitude of the local population in towns and villages, particularly if you are in the enemy's country. Watch all windmills, as they are often used for signals ; also church bells, and clocks on towers. Local inns, barbers' shops, blacksmiths' shops are the usual places for information.

Small children hear and see things, and will usually tell you the truth when their parents won't. Be friendly with the children and seek all information from them possible. When you wish to obtain information, do not ask point-blank questions, but go indirectly to obtain the same, and then put two and two together. When asking questions, appear disinterested ; by this means you can obtain a great deal of information without the individual's knowledge that that is what you are after, and information received in this way is much more valuable than otherwise.

NOTES ON THE COLLECTION AND TRANSMISSION OF INTELLIGENCE BY TROOPS.

Early and complete information regarding any of the enemy's units with which our troops may be engaged is required at all times by the Intelligence Department. This information is obtained by contact with the enemy, and by searching the enemy's dead, wounded, prisoners, and deserters.

You would look for the following identification marks on the German soldiers :—

1. The identity disc, which is hung around the neck.

2. The pay-book, known in German as the *Soldbuch*, is kept in the tunic pocket.

3. The shoulder-strap, which is marked with a number or monogram ; and pay special attention to the colour of these marks, as well as the piping which surrounds it. If you forward the strap in question, state whether taken from the tunic or greatcoat.

4. The markings found on arms, clothing, etc., are inside the flap of the cartridge pouch, on the bayonet near the belt, on the back of the tunic lining, and inside the cap or helmet. The colour of pipings, bands, etc., on the caps. You will find that the band is often covered by a strip of grey cloth, and on the tunics, on the collar and cuffs. Maps, letters, notebooks, orders, etc., are usually found in the skirt pocket at the back of the tunic.

The Procedure in Case of Enemy's Dead.—You will forward to proper authorities, together with a statement as to the place where they were found, all identity discs, papers, and pay-books.

The Procedure in Case of Prisoners.—They are to be searched at the earliest opportunities after capture, in order to prevent them from destroying any letters or orders which may be in their possession. The prisoners will then be sent to Headquarters with the least possible delay. Lightly wounded prisoners fit to be interrogated should accompany the unwounded. The identity discs will be retained by all prisoners, but papers and pay-books will be transmitted together with, but separately from, owners.

The fuzes of exploded shells furnish valuable information. When found, they should be sent to the nearest battery, together with an accurate statement as to the exact location they were found.

Examine all billets and bivouacs deserted by the enemy; likely you will find identification marks, such as chalk marks on the doors. These marks are to be copied and forwarded to the proper authorities.

Captured or abandoned vehicles or horses should be examined for markings, etc.

REPORT WRITING.

The way to write a correct report is very important with a Scout-Sniper. In reporting, like everything else, there is a right way and a wrong way. So many men have obtained such valuable information, but it was rendered useless by not having the time or date on it, or some like mistake. Now, in the remarks of this report you want to put everything in that you think you saw. It does not want to be blurred out like a story-book, but it wants to be short, concise, and to the point. The best way to teach men is to show them the proper way and let them memorize it ; in time it will become second-hand to them. A report should be sent to the O.C. Snipers, and be despatched at the first opportunity. In training a man, after each has written his report, have him read it over, and say to himself : " If I were receiving this message and did not know anything about the conditions, what information would I need before I could act ?" The same then would apply to the Officer to whom he is sending it. By his doing this a great deal of trouble will be saved, and a more intelligent report will be written. The form of the report would be as follows :—

Subject................................*From*

Place ....

To (*Place*) ....*Date* ....

Ref. Map (if necessary)

REMARKS.

Time sent off ....

By whom sent   *Signature*

In describing the following objects, note the kind of information wanted :—

Rivers.—Width, Depth, Fordable, Banks, Bottom, Tidal, whether liable to flood.

Bridges.—Material, Size, Number of Arches, Height, Width of Road, Height of Arch to Level of Water, etc.

ILLUSTRATING HOW CLEARLY SERVICE CAP SHOWS UP ON SKY-LINE.

SHOWING HOW A WELL-CONCEALED POST CAN BE GIVEN AWAY BY TWO PROMINENT LOOPHOLES.

SHOWING THE DANGER OF TAKING BRICKS OUT OF WALLS IN PLAIN VIEW.

Railways.—Gauge, Cutting, Embankment, Bridges, Double or Single Track, etc.

Buildings.—Material, Size, Cellars, Good Field of Fire, etc.

Woods.—Whether passable to all arms.

Obstacles.—Description of same.

Roads.—Width, Class, Metalled or otherwise, Hedges, Ditches, etc.

The battalion that the reporter is writing from or to should never be stated in full, but the code of the same be used—*e.g.* :—

> *From :* 21356 Sniper T. BROWN.
>
> LOB (this representing the unit).
>
> *To :* O.C. Snipers.
>
> LOB.

If this is done in case of capture, the enemy will not know who the troops opposite are ; naturally this is important information, for if there are seasoned troops in the trenches they are far less likely to be active against us than if we had two or three month volunteers ; so if in doubt of being captured, destroy reports. I draw up the following report ; is it right or wrong ?

ENEMY wire.

> *From :* Sniper T. BROWN (names and places to be in block).
>
> LOB.
>
> *To :* O.C. Snipers.
>
> LOB.

LENS $\dfrac{1}{20000}$

No. 2 Sniping Post,

February 2nd, 1917.

Enemy wire cut 45 deg. from this post, for a width of 100 yards, and left of bearing.

Sgt. BROWN,
Sniper No. 2 Post.

D

It is a habit of some men to leave out very important items in their reports. A mistake will give no end of trouble. It is quite unnecessary on an information report to start off " Sir," for it wants to be concise.

You can see the unnecessary work in the following report, the text of which expresses identically the same as above :—

ENEMY wire.

> *From :* 21356 Sniper T. BROWN.
> LOB.
>
> *To :* O.C. Snipers.
> LOB.

LENS $\frac{1}{20000}$

No. 2 Sniping Post,

February 2nd, 1917.

Sir,

While we were out on patrol duty to-night to get information about the enemy's wire, I found that it had been cut for a width of about 100 yards. I went back to my post, and found that the bearings to the right end of the cut was 45 deg.—that is, from No. 2 Post.

4.30 a.m.   Sgt. BROWN.

Sent by Pte. T. DODDS.

Remember, in report writing be clear ; put everything in in as concise a form as possible. All names and places will be written in block letters.

Note.—It is not absolutely necessary to give at the top of the report the name and place of sender, as it is repeated at the close of the message. This can be left to the discretion of the Instructor, but remember, have a uniform system of reporting.

MAP READING.

It will be unnecessary to go into detail on this subject, for there are many books which will clearly explain the same ; but we wish to set forth the practical side of Map Reading, with explanations of the necessary instruments for our work, for it is this practical work which is all that is necessary to the Scout-Sniper, and the rest only tends to confusion.

The first thing to explain to them is the necessity of looking to see if the map covers the area over which they intend to operate. Now, this might seem rather foolish, and it would be in this country, because when we pick up a map our eye automatically picks up the print of some city or town close at hand, which we know well ; but in some foreign parts, where the names are strange to us, this information is going to be harder to find.

Then you want to look for the scale on the map, which will be represented in two ways : (1) By a line divided into equal parts, the construction of which we will explain later ; and (2) by a Representative Fraction, known as the R.F. The R.F. is shown as a fraction, such as $\frac{1}{5000}$. Now, this means that on that particular map 1 inch on the map represents 5,000 inches on the ground. You can see, by having a scale, how easy it is to find the distance between any two points on the map.

To Construct a Scale with a R.F. of $\frac{1}{5000}$.

We know from the R.F. that 1 inch on the map represents 5,000 inches on the ground.

We want a round number, so that the scale can be divided into round equal parts—*e.g.*, 100, 500, etc. Always take 36,000 as the round number, for this equals 1,000 yards (36 inches in a yard).

Now, again, from the R.F. we know that 1 inch on the map represents 5,000 inches on the ground.

D 2

We say to ourselves, How many inches on the map would 36,000 inches on the ground represent ? If 5,000 inches represents 1 inch, 36,000 inches would represent $\frac{36000}{5000} \times 1 = 7 \cdot 2$ inches. Therefore our scale is 7·2 inches long, and represents 36,000 inches, or 1,000 yards. Draw the line, and cut it into ten equal divisions, and each equal division will be 100 yards. You can divide the first division into ten divisions, and each division will be ten yards, etc.

NOTE.—(a) By using the above method, it does away with the confusing method before in use, where a line has to be between 4 inches and 6 inches, etc., and the scale can be worked by a simple division.

(b) Supposing you found by working a R.F. the above way that you only had 1·4 inches, representing 1,000 yards. All you need to do in this case is double or treble, etc., your two figures—e.g. :—

> 1·4 represents 1,000 yards.
>
> 2 × (1·4) represents 2 × (1,000) yards, or 2·8 inches represents 2,000 yards.
>
> or 5 × (1·4) represents 5 × (1,000) yards, or 7 inches represents 5,000 yards, etc. ;

or halve it, as the case may be, to bring it to the convenient length you want.

To cut a Fractional Line into Equal Parts.

To cut B, which is 4·5 inches long, into ten equal parts, or to cut any line into equal parts, draw an auxiliary line, C, any length, but an even number, and divide it into the number of parts that you want AB divided ; join CB, and from divisions on AC draw parallel lines to BC on AB, AB now being cut into the required equal parts.

Above we have explained how to construct a scale knowing the R.F., but it might be necessary at some time to construct a scale in yards of 3 inches to a mile. In this case a little more work is necessary.

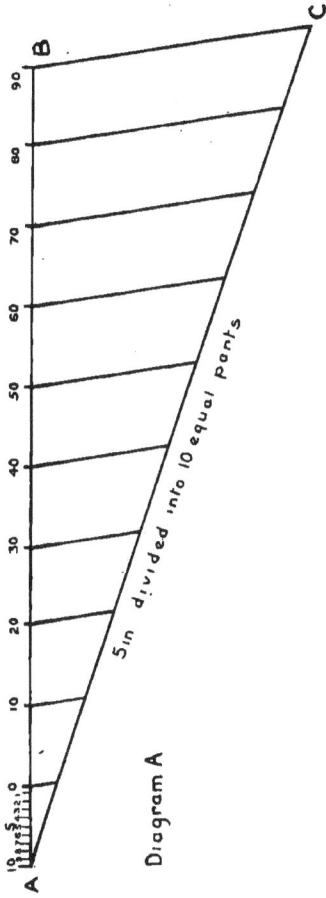

Diagram A

5in divided into 10 equal parts

B

C

5·1 ins.

Divided equally as in diagram A.

In order to solve it by the above simple method, you would have to bring the statement to a R.F.—thus :

3″ to a mile.

In a mile there are 63,360″.

∴ the R.F. is $\frac{3}{63360}$ in. or $\frac{1}{21120}$ in. ;

and it can be worked as above.

The next thing to look for on the map is the North Point and the Variation. On some maps you will find the grid lines are not true ; if this is so, the explanation will be rendered on the map.

It is most important to read all marginal notes, as they contain conventional signs and terms, and full interpretation of the map.

Explain clearly the squaring system, and how easy it is by this method to accurately define location.

Show how to describe points on an unsquared map, the necessity of directing by marked features, and not by lettering. Points would be located by giving range and bearing from above-mentioned marked feature.

Explain clearly the use of the protractor and the compass.

THE MAGNETIC COMPASS.

The magnetic compass consists of three parts :—

1. The Box.
2. The Magnetic Needle.
3. The Card.

The needle, unless otherwise attracted, points to Magnetic North. The compass is divided into 360 parts, called degrees or divisions, shown thus : 360°.

By variation of the compass is meant the number of degrees that the magnetic needle may vary from True North. Roughly speaking, the variation here is 15° West.

The Dip is the tendency which the magnetized point of the magnetic needle has to point downwards. It varies all over the world.

On all maps, sketches, etc., you must show True and Magnetic North lines ; if in a sketch where True North is not at top of a page, it is quite unnecessary to make it so, as long as you place in your True and Magnetic North lines, which are shown thus :—

the magnetic line being headed with an arrow.

There is a Prismatic Mark VII Compass, which likely you will have quite a lot to do with. This is a box compass, with the aid of the prism and phosphorus points for night work. On the side of the box there are the degrees marked in tens, but leaving the unit off to save space, 10 representing 100, etc. ; and there is a disc around the top of the box which revolves. You will notice a phosphorus point on the glass of this disc, and also a nitch in line with it on the side ; there is a screw on the side to hold disc steady, also a pin to steady the needle disc. Along the cover there is a thread line with phosphorescence at each end. To take a bearing by day on an object : For example, let us take a bearing on a tree. Raise the compass to the eye, letting it lay in the fingers, and being steadied by the thumb (by use of thumb-ring), and look through the prism. You align your sight as you would through a rifle, from the eye through the prism as a backsight,

along the hair-line on the cover as a foresight to the
tree which is the object. When the needle disc—for
the disc and needle are combined—steadies, the angle
which is reflected to the eye through the prism can be
read. As to its benefit to night work : Supposing you
took a bearing by day, or took a bearing on the map

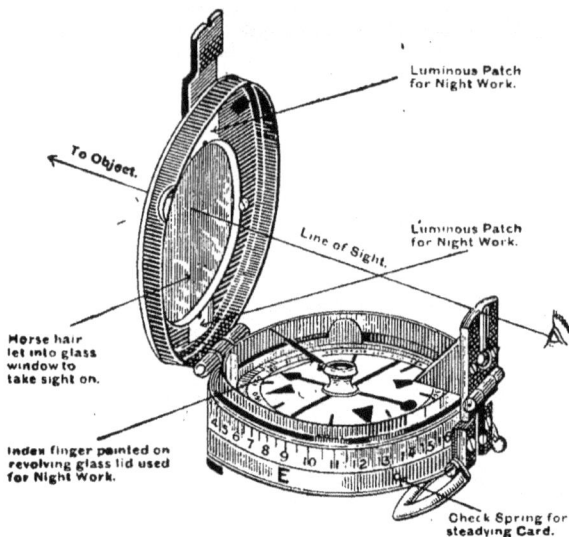

Luminous Patch
for Night Work.

To Object.

Luminous Patch
for Night Work.

Line of Sight.

Horse hair
let into glass
window to
take sight on.

Index finger pointed on
revolving glass lid used
for Night Work.

Check Spring for
steadying Card.

The Service Luminous Prismatic Compass.

from one point to another, that you wanted to move
upon by night, you would proceed as follows :—Let
us take 280° as the bearing. You would loosen the
disc screw in the side, and turn the disc until the phosphorescence on the glass and nitch points to 23 on the
side. Then tighten the screw again. To march on
your point by night, as long as the magnetized end on

the magnetic needle points to the phosphorescence on the disc, nitch, and 23, the direction in which you move is the way the phosphorescence points along the hair-line on the cover. You will then be marching on a bearing of 230°. It is unnecessary to hold the compass continually in your hand and keeping the magnetic point pointing to 23 on the side. Look along the thread-line and see some object, a tree or something in its line, close the compass, and march on that ; then take another bearing, and so on. (See diagram.)

NOTE.—If you take a bearing with the compass, remember that it is a magnetic bearing. If you wished to use that bearing to work localities on the map, you would use the protractor, which is true bearing ; so keep in mind the following rule :—

> Magnetic to True=Subtract Variation.
> True to Magnetic=Add Variation.

Work out a few problems on the visibility of points from the map you are using, until you are perfectly satisfied that your class can easily and accurately figure whether one point can be seen from another.

Following the above instructions, give the class a series of practical problems to work out, based on the following lines :—

To find your Position on the Map.

1. *With the Compass.*—Take bearings on two easily recognized landmarks which are marked on the map.

To find the " back or reverse " bearing, you proceed as follows :—

If your bearing to the object is over 180°, you subtract 180° to find back bearing.

If your bearing to the object is less than 180°, you add 180°.

Having found your two bearings and calculated your reverse bearings, plot these from their respective objects, and where the two lines intersect is your position on the map.

NOTE.—To plot, you will use the protractor, so it will be necessary, because of your bearings being taken with the compass being magnetic, to bring them to True. Remember :—

> Magnetic to True=Subtract Variation.
> True to Magnetic=Add Variation.

2. *Without a Compass.*—Resection : By the use of a piece of thin paper. Take any point, and from that point draw straight lines to natural objects which are also marked on the map from your position.

Lay the paper on the map, so that the lines, three or more, point in the direction of the marked features; then, again, the point of intersection is your position.

Reproduce map sheet $\frac{1}{20000}$.

We take a bearing on *H2d* 22, 53, W. corner of Bartholomew's Wood, and find it to be 37° Magnetic, True bearing 22°. Reverse bearing, $22°+180°=202°$ T.

We take a bearing on *H2a* 62, 90, junction of footpaths, and find it to be 6° 30′ Magnetic or 351° 30′ True. Reverse bearing, 171° 30′ T.

Taking the above reverse bearings from their respective objects on the map, and drawing lines from same, we find that the lines intersect at *H8a* 91, 71, corner of hedge. This is my position.

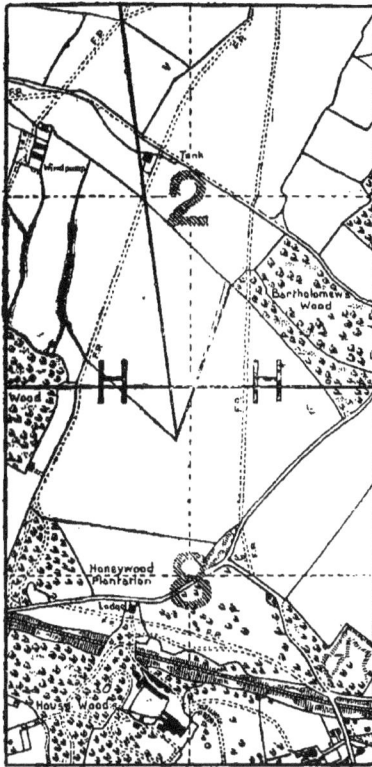

Then work out some problems based on the map
you are using, such as—

1. Finding distance by road from one point to
another.

2. Finding ranges from one point to another.

3. You observe from (give map location) enemy
working party at (give map location). What steps

would you take to get a machine-gun in action situated in our lines at (give map location), assuming that contour level of working party and machine-gun are the same, and that target is invisible from machine-gun, but no obstruction to course of bullet; also assuming that you have a map protractor and compass, but that the N.C.O. in charge of machine-gun has none of these instruments, and the machine-gun Officer in charge is not present. Give figures.

This necessitates your taking bearing with the protractor from gun to object, and bringing bearing to Magnetic North for the purpose of setting the gun and ascertaining range, etc.

4. Set compass for night marching to march from one point to another. Take bearing from the map. This necessitates changing the protractor bearing to a compass bearing that is true to Magnetic, and setting the compass.

5. You observe from (give map location) and from (give map location) a trench mortar. The bearing from the first is —— Magnetic, and from the second point —— Magnetic. Give map location of trench mortar, etc.

6. What steps would you take to ensure reaching your exact objective if portion in enemy's position you were ordered to take extended from —— to ——, and your jumping-off point extended from —— to ——, assuming country is new to you and the attack is at night? Give figures. This necessitates ranges and flank bearings for the use of guides.

7. Give questions on visibility of points.

8. Panoramic sketches to show locations, etc.

Have your class taken maps outside and identified natural features with marked features on the map, etc.?

THREE WAYS OF FINDING TRUE NORTH.

Without the use of the compass we will give you three ways of finding True North. Of course, those men who come from the backwoods, and know direction by growth, trees, etc., it would be very hard to lose them ; but the following must be taught, and will likely be very helpful to you at some time, when lost without a compass. A person need not be told—at least, we take it so—if you were lost in a dense wood, the first thing to do would be to climb a high tree and look around. Nevertheless, the first way is by means of the sun, which at noon is due South, and North will be directly opposite. The second way is by means of the watch method. If your watch is correct, point the hour hand at the sun, bisect a line through the centre between that and twelve o'clock, and that line runs North and South, the line running away from the sun being North. (See diagram.)

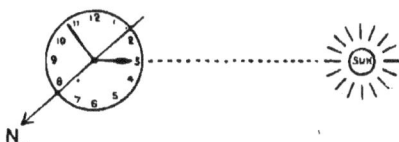

The third way is by means of the Pole or North Star. The diagram will show you its position with respect to the Big Bear or Dipper.

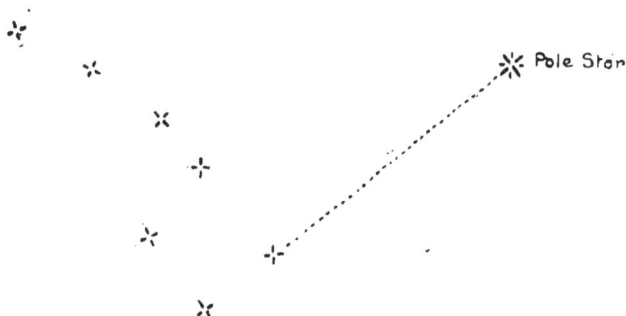

Pole Star

THERE ARE TWO WAYS OF SETTING A MAP.

1. By the compass.

2. By marked features on the map corresponding to natural features on the ground.

To Set a Map by Means of the Compass.—Place the compass on the map, on the marked Magnetic North line, and turn the map until the magnetized point of the magnetic needle corresponds with the marked Magnetic North on your map. Then your map is set.

If you were without a compass, you could set a map by corresponding marked features on the map with the corresponding natural features on the ground. For example, if you were standing on a road which led to a certain town, turn the map until the road on the map is parallel with the road that you are on, and pointing to the town ; then your map is set. Or, again, if you could see a church half-left which was represented on the map, and a house quarter-right, turn the map till the church on same pointed to the actual church, and the house on the map pointed to the actual house. Then, again, your map is set.

PLATE I.

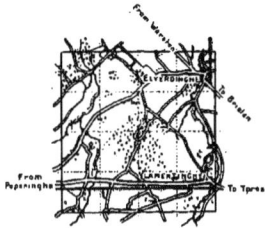

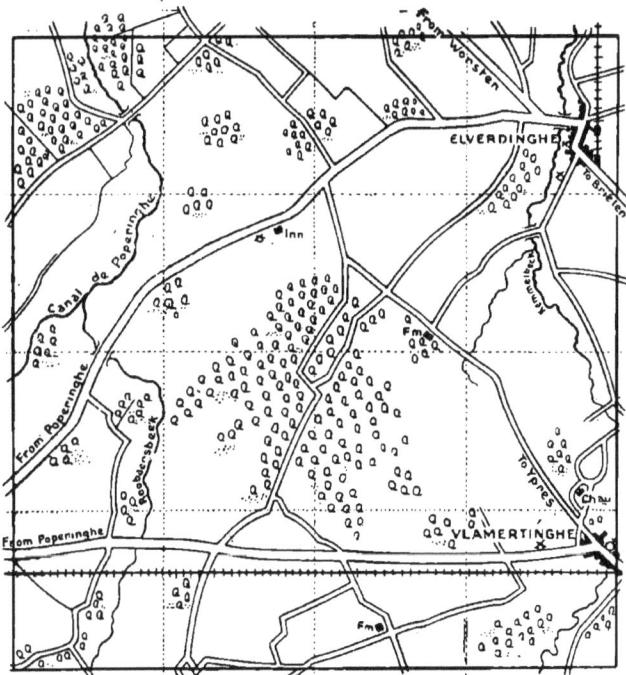

ENLARGING.

You can copy, enlarge, or reduce maps by the square system. (See diagram.) Supposing that you wanted to copy 2 square inches on a map which was 1 inch to the mile, or $\frac{1}{63360}$ four times. To do this divide your small map into squares, and draw another square four times as large, and divide into smaller squares similarly to the first; then your objects will cut the lines of the larger squares in the corresponding same place as the smaller, and your map will be enlarged.

To find Length of Sides from R.F.—A map has a R.F. of $\frac{1}{800}$; a copy is required, and on a scale of $\frac{1}{400}$. Measure the longer side of the map, and say, for instance, that it is 4 inches long. Then :—

$$\frac{1}{800} : \frac{1}{400} = 4 : x.$$
$$\frac{x}{800} = \frac{4}{400}$$
$$400x = 3200.$$
$$x = 8 \text{ inches.}$$

Then draw the sides and the minor squares, and continue as above.

CONTOURS.

As contours are very important, let us make a study of them. You know now the definition of a contour, but that is about all. You know that the V.I. is always the same, but the H.E. varies. To exemplify more clearly, but on a smaller scale, let us draw the contour lines of a rubber boot. The lines to be drawn with a V.I. of 6 inches (in maps the V.I. is usually 5, 10, 50, and 100 feet). If you picture the boot, you will know that contour around the bottom will be differently shaped to the contour line around the top, although the depth of lines above each other are the same. So it is with natural features; one contour line may be drawn including a re-entrant, the line above it might not include the re-entrant, and so on.

THREE MEN DRESSED TO CONFORM TO LOCAL CONDITIONS.
Notice the unnatural effect of flowers in cap of man to right of sergeant. This picture was taken at the recruits' first attempt at concealment. They used the flowers for head covering to conform with the surrounding conditions, but in No. 1 you will note that he shows part of his body, as indicated by the arrow. In No. 2 a part of his cap shows, and in No. 3 you will note that the flowers are partly withered, and, being unnatural, do not conform to the freshness and lay-out of the other flowers close at hand.

In this picture three men are concealed not 10 feet from the camera, and are impossible to see, which clearly shows how easy it is to hide yourself by the proper use of the natural features.

SHOWING THE REFLECTION OF THE SUN ON THE SIGHTS AND MUZZLE OF THE RIFLE.
It is not only from a loophole that the reflection of the sun on parts of the rifle will give away your position. In this case you can see the reflection of the sun on the sights and muzzle indicated by an arrow. Accurate firing can be done just as easily by stepping back and firing through the branches.

SHOWING HOW THE SKIN AND SERVICE CAP SHOW UP.

Supposing that a hill is represented by five contour lines, and the V.I. was 10 feet, that hill must be 50 feet or over, but under 60 feet ; for if it were 60 feet or over, and under 70 feet, it would be represented by six contours.

By contour lines we can always tell the slope of a hill, whether gradual or otherwise, knowing the scale of the map. Let us take five contour lines, the V.I. being 100 feet, and we want to know the slope from *A* to *B* (see diagram). Join *AB*, draw parallel lines with equal distances between to represent the V.I. (above), and make them to represent the contours, and draw perpendicular lines from *AB* up to the respective heights.

These heights are marked on the parallel, and equal distance between lines above.

In diagram, notice that contour lines close together denote steepness, whereby contour lines farther apart are less steep. That is quite easy to see, for on one side there is 400 feet rise to a mile, and on the other 300 feet to less than half a mile. In this case the distance of the rise being found from the scale.

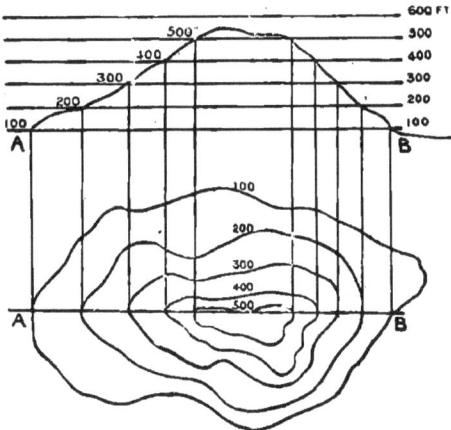

E

DEFINITIONS.

HILL	.. Is high ground that falls away from every side.
BASIN	.. A small area of level ground surrounded by hills; also the district drained by a river. Think of the depression in a wash-basin.
CREST	.. The edge of a top of hill or a mountain, the position of which a gentle slope changes to an abrupt one. The top of a bluff or cliff.
COL	.. A depression between two adjacent mountains or hills, or a neck of land that connects an outlying feature with a range of mountains or hills, or with a spurt.
KNOLL	.. A low, detached hill.
PLATEAU	.. A flat surface on the top of a hill; an elevated plane.
A RAVINE	.. A narrow valley with steep sides.
SALIENT	.. A projection from the side of a hill or mountain, running out and down from the main feature.
RE-ENTRANT	.. Is where the hillside is curved inwards towards the main feature. This is always found between two salients.
TABLELAND	.. A high-lying, level district of country.
UNDER-FEATURE	A minor feature; an offspring of a main feature.
UNDULATING GROUND	.. Is ground consisting of alternate gentle elevations and depressions.

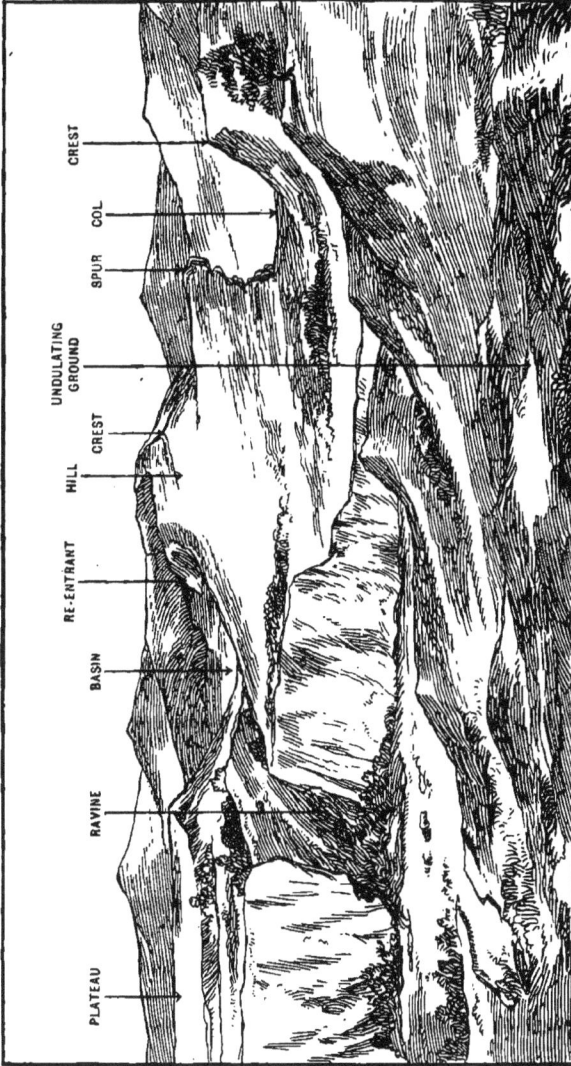

CREST

COL

SPUR

UNDULATING
GROUND

CREST

HILL

RE-ENTRANT

BASIN

RAVINE

PLATEAU

DEFINITIONS EXPLAINED

CONTOUR ... An imaginary line running along the
surface of the ground at the same
height above mean sea level throughout its length ; each contour represents a fixed rise or fall from the
ones next to it. These are ex-
pressed in feet. This fixed rise or
fall is known as the V.I., or the
Vertical Interval.

HORIZONTAL
EQUIVALENT.. Or H.E., is the horizontal distance
in which a given difference of level
will occur at a given degree of slope,
always stated in yards ; it is the
distance in yards between two
contours on a map. (See diagram.)

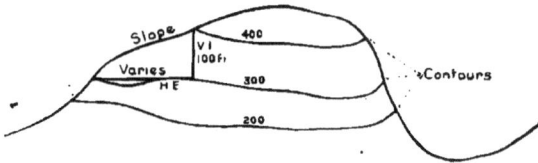

TRAVERSING.

To traverse a compass is essential. Traversing
enables you to plot and sketch your trench system,
or enables you to map any area of open country. It
is done by a series of straight lines, by taking bearings
in each turn. In obtaining the information, you use
a chain line (see diagram), marking in all details on each
side, giving bearing to each, if necessary. This work
is very interesting, and with a little practice the greatest
accuracy can be obtained. The procedure is as follows : In this case we start with a hill overlooking a
station (1), with a circle around ; it is shown in the
chain line, and means the starting-point. We take
a bearing on the station, and find it to be 271°, so
we mark it in. Now we advance in a straight line

BEARING
ON HILL
FROM ROAD

PLATE IV.

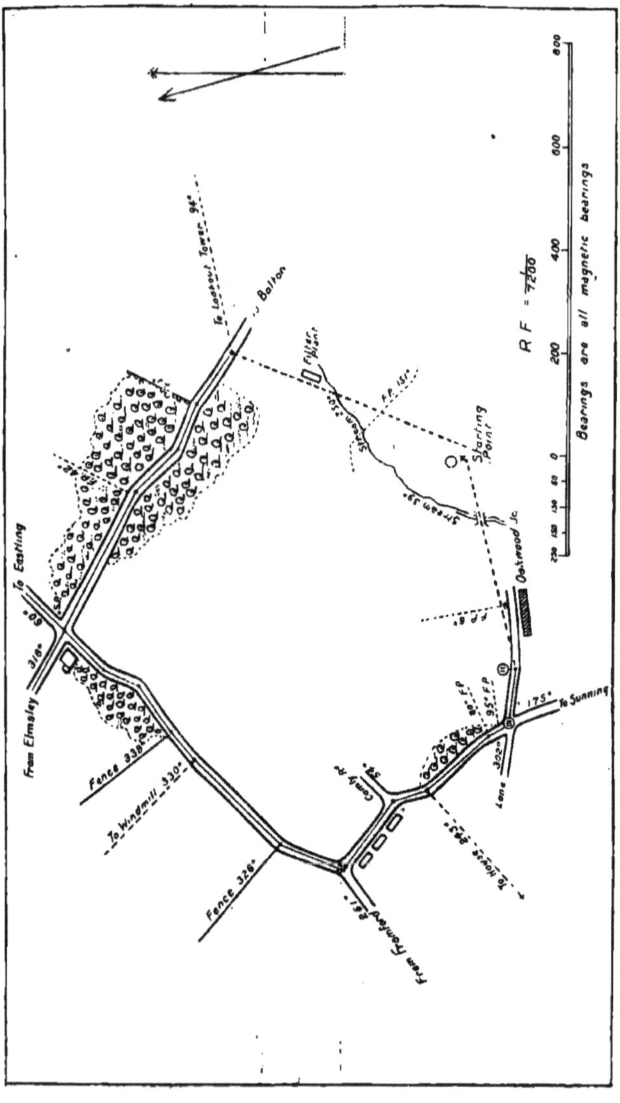
To Eastling
From Elmsley
318°
Fence 338°
To Windmill 330°
Fence 326°
To Lookout Tower 94°
Bolton
Filter Plant
Starting Point
Stream 39°
Oatwood Jc.
To Sunning
175°
332°
Lane
To House 285°
R F = 1/7200
Bearings are all magnetic bearings

towards the station, counting out paces, and stopping
at every place that we want to mark in any information, either on the right or left of our line. In this
case we proceed 110 paces, and find a stream crossing
our line, the bearing in the direction that it flows
being 39°; so we fill 110 in our chain line, and the
stream on the right with a bearing of the same. We
now take up our counting from 110 paces, and continue
on—for example, 110, 111. Our next point is 385
paces, where we find a station on the left; we fill in
the number of paces from the road the station is, etc.
Here we also find a footpath going off at an angle of
106° on the right of the road; this is also filled in.
Then we continue on to 420 paces, the point to which
we took our bearing. Here we draw a line across the
chain line, and take a new bearing along the road
which we find ourselves on; we number this point (2)
and fill in the new bearing up the road as far as we can
see, which is the point at which the road branches off.
We take 130 paces to the point our bearing was taken
on, and find nothing of interest which we wish to mark
in; so at this point we take new bearings, and call
it (3), and continue on, etc. The chain line and plot
in the diagram is completed. This is the work of a
man who has had no previous instruction, and is accurate except for the matter of a degree or so. Attached
are also plots of men under instruction; these plots
were taken from a chain line, as explained above.

To Plot.—Make a scale; in this scale it is 200 paces
to the inch. Place your conventional sign for Magnetic and True North; then from your starting-point
take a bearing of 271°, and the line will be a little over
2 inches long, for your first bearing consisted of 410
paces. Then fill in objects, etc., that you have
taken note of, according to scale, such as stream, a
little (⅓ inch) from starting-point—for it is 110 paces—
and draw stream at the given bearing from your line.
You continue this throughout.

Traversing is an excellent means to show quickly
your exact location.

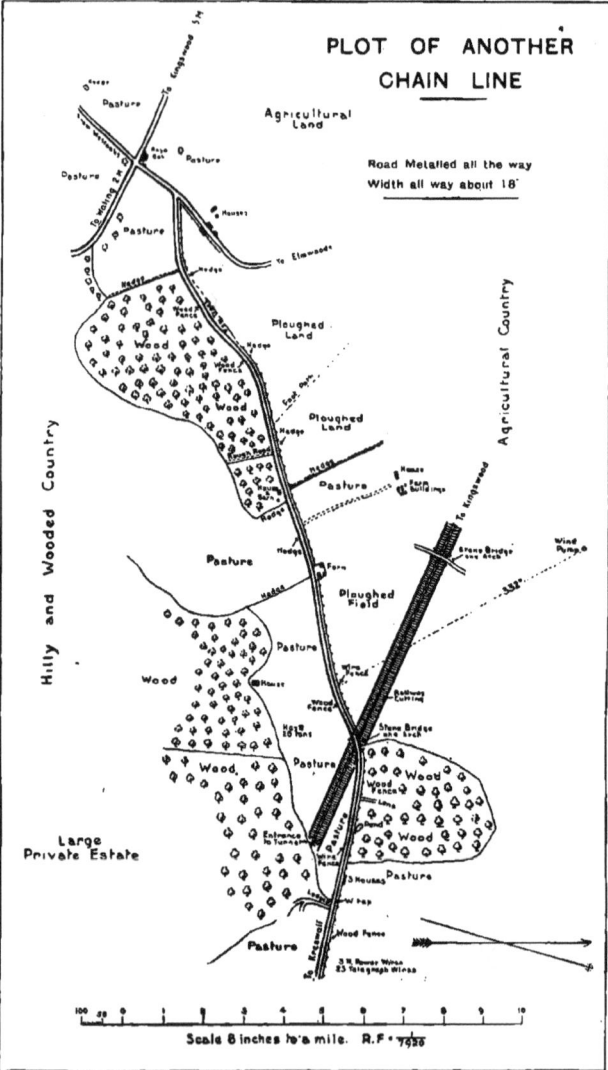

PLOT OF ANOTHER
CHAIN LINE

Road Metalled all the way
Width all way about 18'

Agricultural Land

Hilly and Wooded Country

Agricultural Country

Wood

Ploughed Land

Ploughed Land

Pasture

Pasture

Ploughed Field

Wood

Pasture

Wood

Pasture

Wood

Large Private Estate

Wood

Pasture

Pasture

Scale 8 inches to a mile. R.F = 1/7920

OBSERVATION OF GROUND.

One of the duties of a Scout-Sniper is observation. He wants to be trained at home before going abroad— the importance of continual and systematic observation; a man sees something, but does not see everything. Your memory wants to be trained to work with your observations. You have noticed a person take out his watch and look at the time, and put his watch back in his pocket again. A half-minute later, when you ask him the time, he again will take the watch out of his pocket and look; that is nothing but carelessness. Now is the time to train yourself to think and use your memory.

In observation of ground every detail should be observed and carefully watched. There are two ways of observing—with the naked eye, and with the eye plus magnetic power, such as with the field-glasses, telescope, etc. As we have said before, you must train yourself to systematic observation. You must slowly and carefully study your sector. Many men foolishly traverse their telescope as they would a machine-gun, in order to have their whole front always under observation, not realizing that they have just their own sector to watch; the other posts will look after themselves. Again, any person can look through a telescope, but very few are capable of using this instrument to the best advantage. You want to locate and find, and in order to do this your telescope should be traversed methodically and deliberately over the area under observation. This insures that no part of your front is missed or slurred over. Any object that seems unnatural should be subjected to the closest possible scrutiny. The easiest form of telescopic work is searching a parapet, for here the area to be kept under observation is small; and after scrutinizing carefully its outline, colour is usually detected. To attain this, almost instant spotting should be the aim of all instruction. In order to train your men in this, place out four or five objects, two or three of which are easy to pick up, the other two less easy. Then have your men search for them with telescopes. In observing for movement, and you think you see something move in a certain spot, do not look straight at it, but two or three yards to the right or left, for the centre of the eye is less perceptible than the sides. As for the glasses, learn to know your focus and to focus quickly ; a little mark can be put on the field-glass or telescope at your focus, so that no time will be lost in focussing. Practise quickness in finding your object, taking the necessary care, thoroughness of examination, and systematic covering. When you have found an object, note the following :—Size, nature, outline, colour, position in reference to surrounding objects, and description of same. On the Standard signaller's telescope there is a high-powered lens attached, which can be used according to weather conditions. These lenses are marked on the eyepiece with an H. or L., meaning High or Low power.

Take your men out on observation marches ; have them take a notebook and pencil, and jot down all observations. The more practice that they have in this, the more efficient observers they become.

JUDGING DISTANCE.

It is easy for a man to train himself to become very accurate at judging distance. It is surprising how efficient a man becomes with a little training. You want to take him out, and have him judge under different natural and climatic conditions.

Most men know the length of a football field ; comparison might aid them to more accurate figures. In recruits' judging, do not let them judge over 600 yards ; when they become efficient up to that, it will be all right to increase their range. From " Musketry Regulations " we find that—

Objects are Overestimated—

When kneeling or lying.
When both background and object are of similar colour.

On broken ground.

When looking over a valley or undulating ground.

In avenues, long streets, or ravines.

When the object lies in the shade.

When the object is viewed in mist or failing light.

When the object is only partially seen.

When the heat is rising from the ground.

Objects are Underestimated—

When the sun is behind the observer.

In bright light or clear atmosphere.

When both background and object are of different colour.

When the intervening ground is level or covered with snow.

When looking over water or a deep chasm.

When looking upward or downward.

When the object is large.

Good practice for judging distance is to send out fatigue men to given distances, and have the squad judge their distance. Have them notice the difference when men are lying down, kneeling, and standing up, at different ranges. A good and fairly accurate way is to judge the maximum and the minimum distance that the object could possibly be away from you and take the mean. For example, it is 200 yards at the most, and 100 yards at the least ; the mean would be $100+200$ over 2, or 150 yards. Rough guessing must be avoided, and disciplinary action must be taken against any soldier so inclined.

SNIPING POSTS.

Men must be thoroughly trained at choosing and digging posts at home before going abroad. Your training ground wants to be in a part of the country where the natural features vary, where there are old houses, hedges, undulating and level ground, etc. The front abroad is wide ; therefore you want to train your men under as many different circumstances as possible.

After you have lectured them on the important things they must know, such as the compass, map-reading, traversing, and have had several observation walks upon which you showed them likely places for posts, and explained why they are likely places, then is the time to take them out and give them a radius of, say, 2 miles, and let them thoroughly examine the ground, choose and dig their posts. They must be reminded that though they are digging at home here, they must consider their having an enemy. They must consider the whereabouts of the enemy's trenches, and to what flank it is most convenient for him to fire. Upon taking up their posts, bearings must be taken on two prominent landmarks—two, if possible, that are marked on the map—also from what point he got up to his post, and could he do so if he advanced on it some dark night. If possible, have them draw a sketch of the front. When completed, have them view their front as the enemy would see it. If it is in the open, remember, do not make your trap-door too large, and do not forget to protect the sods. Do not throw the earth all over the place, for if you do it will be readily seen by the enemy. Take a blanket or something out, and lay the earth on the same, and carry it away to some unseen spot, so that the natural features will not be disturbed. We noticed a lot of Imperials on Salisbury Plain making really excellent posts, but spoiling them by moving continually around the front to see how they looked from the enemy's point of view, causing a track to be made. Remember, the post must be dug and concealed so carefully that, when completed, a person could be 3 feet away and not notice it ; for this reason the natural features must not be disturbed in the least. Your suspicion is aroused if at some dawn you notice even gorse cut in No Man's Land, so will the enemy's ; so take the greatest care not to disturb the natural features. We have seen gorse placed in front of a loophole to hide the flash ; the idea is all right, but if you do this you must remember that unless this is continually changed, that gorse is going to die. The colour will change, and perhaps give away your post.

When the post is completed to the satisfaction of the men who are going to man it—this is in training— they should occupy it at once, and construct range-cards of the front as seen through the loophole. The range-card will be hung just below the loophole plate, as per diagram (see pages 106-108), in order that it is before you at all times. A report on his sector should be made.

On the completion of these posts, an Officer should go around, taking the whole of his class, and criticize the mistakes made. Now is the time for the men to ask their questions ; the more questions they ask, and the better their answers, the better the class will get on. Go through everything, leaving no point untouched.

Upon the completion of the Officer's criticism, the men will be much more associated with what to do next time ; so give them another area, and let them start again. If they wish to arrange their plan of post, let them do so, but remember, severely reprimand the man who makes the same mistake twice. This is only due to carelessness. Keep them at these posts until they are completed to your satisfaction ; following that, you give them some night work until they get used to the dark, and then have them dig by night, having planned their post position, etc., by day through periscope or telescope. While digging at night, have half the class out in search of them. Remember that on a clear night, unless you are very quiet, your pick or shovel will give you away. At the post, while one is digging, have one man out 3 or 4 yards on guard, to see that you are not discovered.

It has come to the notice of men occupying a Sniping Post that the effect of the Snipers' firing interferes with the observations of the observer due to the discharge of the rifle. In this case it would be advantageous to have a partition between the two in order that the observer will not be affected in any way with his systematic observations. A tube arrangement could be arranged between the observer and Sniper so that the observer's observation can be immediately signalled to the firer.

If in the front line, it is better that the Sniper and observer should have separate posts about 5 or 6 feet apart, communicated between by the above method.

HOW TO TAKE ADVANTAGE OF, AND OCCUPY, NATURAL COVER:

Take your men out, and train them thoroughly how to take advantage of cover, gorse, mounds, hedges, etc. Many is the time that we have seen infantry training in extended order. When the whistle was sounded for " Down," the men would just fall, paying no attention whatever to the natural cover that would conceal them. This is a great mistake. We have had fifty men down in an open field not 20 yards away from us absolutely invisible ; they used their brains, and showed adaptability. Other men that were sent out within the given range could not hide themselves at all. In order that these men do this properly, it is due to the Officer to take them out and explain the important points, in the use of cover, and how to adapt themselves to the same. The man should not hesitate to place green grass in the front of his hat, etc., if he thinks that he will be less likely seen.

At a great many different surroundings the question is asked at a distance of 200 yards, Can a man lay down and not be seen if he lays perfectly still ? While under these conditions he can observe more or less, but he can't shoot or move without detection. On taking advantage of cover, you must use every effort to conform to local conditions. You must have no wire around the top of your Service cap. You must

have a veil or mask over your face ; cover your head
with the same material if you take your cap off. You
must also wear gloves ; woollen khaki ones are the best.
If in summer and too warm, cover your hands with
the same material as your veil. Your buttons must
be painted, or covered with a khaki-covered material.
Your front buttons can be covered with a 2-inch strip
of khaki cloth pinned on with safety-pins. Your
pocket and shoulder-strap buttons can be unbuttoned
and pinned down over buttons with a few black safety-
pins. In fact, you can do the same with the front of
your Service jacket if a strip of cloth is not obtainable.
We should strongly recommend that all Snipers should
be supplied with brown leather buttons. Black ammunition boots will give you away if you are not careful.
Your rifle must be painted to suit the surrounding
conditions. When out stalking, you may have to
leave your pack and some of your other equipment
behind. You can in some cases stick small branches
with leaves on in your belt. When stalking, it is most
important to watch your flanks as well as your front.
It does not matter how well you are hidden from front
view if you are caught from one of your flanks. You
can crawl through long grass and standing grain or
corn, when there is a wind blowing, without detection ;
you might also be able to shoot from such cover ; if
so, always choose a forward natural slope. While
firing from a concealed post or natural cover, fairly
close to the enemy's lines, you must work the bolt
of your rifle with great care, as the sound of your bolt
is easier to locate than the sound of your rifle fire ;
also, in an open post or natural cover, the empty cartridge cases ejected into the air may glitter in the sun,
and may be seen by a close observer. You will rarely
have to fire rapid unless an attack is on, and then in
the din of battle it does not matter so much. Your
main point is to be able to fire one shot, or your first
shot, quick and accurate. When there is no wind,
and you creep through a field of standing grain or
grass, a keen observer will soon see the unnatural

movement of the same ; and if you put your head up,
it is like putting your head out of water—easily seen.
You might fire from a forward slope of a grass or grain
field if you are not so close to the enemy that he can
see the grain moving from the blast of the discharge.
In occupying any cover, be careful of your background. Never shoot from, or occupy, the top of a
large lone tree. It might in some cases be all right
for observation if you or nobody else is shooting in
the neighbourhood. The same way, if you are shooting
from a forest, choose the least conspicuous tree, and
keep away from the first line of trees. Never shoot
out of the top of a tree from the side nearest to the
enemy ; the blast from the discharge of your rifle will
give you away when it is calm, and the opening and
closing of the branches caused by the wind will expose
you to a keen observer. Never have a wall for a close
background, as an enfiladed bullet, in particular, might
glance and kill you. Also, be very careful of metal
roads for a background ; the road may give you a
silhouette effect, and when in front the bullet will
ricochet and the stones will fly, with perhaps fatal
results. The above is really a good place to keep
away from. The enemy have also the range exactly
of all roads and railways.

Look out for the enemy aircraft. If shooting from
a room in a house, and the wall behind is not too far
away from the window, make a row of small holes at
a height to suit you on this inner wall, so as to get at
different angles when shooting. Of course, you shoot
from the other side of the wall, and in this case you
can put your rifle a few inches through it. If they
shoot in through the window, they are not likely to
hit you through any of these small holes on this inner
wall, but in this case you must cover up any window
or door that might happen to be behind you. The
room does not necessarily need to be dark, but you
must have no silhouette effect by having an opening
direct in your rear. You can also cut a hole in the

SEVEN MEN IN LINE IN A POSITION TO OBSERVE ON SHOOT, TAKEN 15 FEET AWAY.
This picture illustrates how easy it is, even in the open, to conceal men. In this case grass is the only means of protection, but you will notice how much more difficult it is for the enemy to find you, if the growth of the immediate vicinity is used for body cover. Arrows indicate the position of the men in the prone position.

NOTE MAN IN PRONE POSITION APPEARING AS A SMALL BUSH.

A SNIPING POST WITH RIFLE PROTRUDING.

This picture shows what an organized and concealed sniping post looks like from the front. This post, as explained in the notes, will comfortably hold two or three men. The object to note here is the reflection of the sun on the foresight of the rifle protruding, which is shown to the right of the cross, thus showing the necessity of holding the rifle well back.

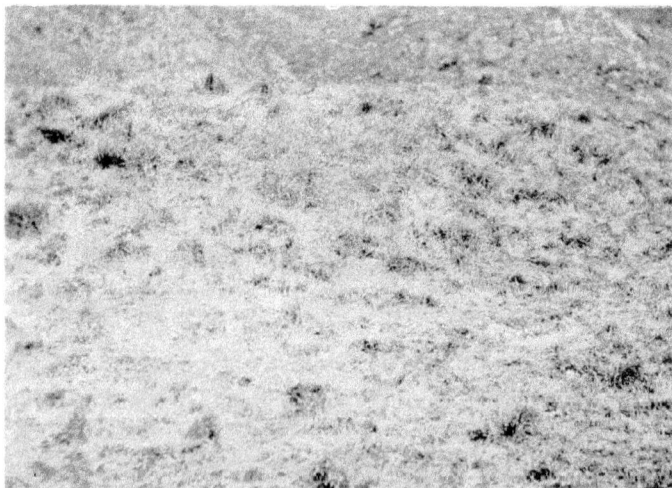

SAME SNIPING POST WHEN PROPERLY USED.

Picture as above, but with the rifle withdrawn the Sniper can fire as freely and see just as well, at the same time making it impossible for the enemy to locate him.

outside wall to shoot through, but never let your rifle protrude. If even half a brick is missing in a wall, it is easily noted—at any rate, easily seen—and if any bullets are coming from your direction, he will likely shoot at it. A good shot with a good telescopic sight will be more or less successful to 400 or 500 yards. In many cases like this there are orchards or other trees around the houses which will conceal the flash, etc. In using telescopes or field-glasses, be careful that the sun does not make a heliograph of your lens and give your position away. The same care must be taken in using your watch and compass, even your pocket or Service issue knife, or any other bright article must be handled with care, when the sun might reflect your whereabouts. A ring on your finger might give you away also. You must learn to move slowly and evenly over comparatively open ground, so that your movements cannot be detected.

In connection with this work, all Snipers, when in billets behind the lines or before going to the front, should constantly practise themselves in this work. Put one party against each other ; get around and through each other's lines without being seen or heard. In England we should use blank ammunition for this work. Tell them not to shoot unless they see somebody with a reasonable chance to make a good hit, and it is surprising how little ammunition these men will use. In France it may not be practicable while practising in rear of lines to fire blank ammunition, but it would work out nicely in the following manner : If you see a man, cover him with your rifle—be careful that it is not loaded—and walk straight to where he is. If they both see each other, the one that gets up first or challenges the other first wins, and the loser will come over and work with the other party. The two go far enough back to get cover to deploy, so they will not be seen in the same place again, and then proceed cautiously forward and continue the practice. On the other hand, if you thought you saw a man, and

F

went over and found you were mistaken, you become the prisoner of the other party, and start to work with them. It is surprising how quickly they get on with this work, and how keen observers they become in a very short time. It seems that after a few practices nothing escapes their notice. They begin with watching their front only, but in a short time they watch in every direction. Practise visual training, letting a few men hide inside a given area, and have the class turn their backs on them ; when ready, they turn about, and everybody tries to locate someone. If not successful, advance 50 yards, and so on, until you locate them all. Always impress upon them the necessity of quick action and decision.

HOW AND WHERE TO CONSTRUCT ARTIFICIAL COVER.

For Snipers and the Use of Same.

Neither as to the methods of construction nor as to the location of artificial cover for Sniping Posts can any hard or fast rules be laid down, as there is such a vast difference with regard to local conditions. What would be the best place in one case would be useless in another.

Before you can construct an artificial Sniping Post you must have a certain amount of natural cover to begin with, unless it is in your fire trenches, but even in that case there must be no fresh visible work done on the forward side of the fire trench.

When operating from the fire trenches or parados the following will be of great value : Outer face of fire trench should be as irregular as possible, both as regards forward front slope and top of parapet. Have strewn about the forward slope of trench pieces of board, sticks, small brush, empty bottles, empty bully beef and jam tins (these should be first cleaned for sanitary reasons)—in fact, all other odds and ends that you have no further use for. You can tunnel inside of trench for concealed loopholes. An old cap over your loophole on outside of parapet, with a small hole in top of same for looking through, will make a good Observation Post. You can make a nice place to shoot from by placing a bully beef tin or jam tin over your loophole. To make this successfully you must have several other tins lying around ; this kind of work must be done gradually.

You can also, on any forward or grassy slope on parapet or elsewhere, construct a wooden trap-door or hinge ; on this door place about two inches of green sod, same as surroundings. Sod can be fastened to trap-door with long nails, and keep watered or renewed to assimilate the surroundings ; it can be opened very gradually for shooting and observing. You can also line half a sandbag with wire-screening to hold it in shape ; place it between the other sandbags. If well done, it will defy all detection. Very small holes will do for observation. The enemy practise all sorts of tricks, and has all kinds of rubbish on the forward slopes of his trenches—old beams, brick, pieces of furniture, old mattresses, etc. They have not got all that rubbish there for in any way to strengthen their works, but it is to shoot and observe from. You must shoot into all these things from time to time, but be very careful that the enemy does not do it to you first.

The best place for concealed Sniping Posts is in front of our fire trenches, if local conditions will allow as to space between ours and enemy trenches. Where trenches are close together and the ground in the rear is too low, the last and only choice is in our own front line.

A Sniping Post should not be located in the trenches if there is any way of helping it. It would be better, perhaps, if the enemy trenches were too

close to locate it, say, 10 yards in front of our own
trenches, and to tunnel to it, because when there is
shooting going on the enemy will look for it coming
from our own trench. If the trenches are only 50
or 60 yards apart, a post can still be constructed a
few yards in front, with small loopholes out through
a bunch of rank weeds or a small forward slope, and
be·effectively concealed even at this short range.   If
the water is not too near the surface to make tunnel-
ing difficult, it can still be done by digging pretty
well down.   Make a kind of shallow well inside your
trench, and start a few feet from the bottom of same,
and tunnel on an upward slope, drain back into the
well and pump out from there.   While this can be
done all right, there is no use doing it if other suitable positions requiring less work and maintenance
can be found.   You also at this short range take a
chance of being undermined and being blown up.
But the greatest objection of a post so close to the
enemy's lines is that you only cover such a narrow
front of his trenches, unless you have loopholes at
several different angles.   It is also better to have a
longer range.   If you can occupy a higher position
you could look into and behind the enemy lines.
The parados should also be considered in locating a
Sniping Post, and it gives you a more commanding
position than in the parapet.   In places where
trenches are only 20 and 30 yards apart it is not
practicable to fire from your own front trenches,
but in rear of same, if the ground slope makes it
possible.   Now, to protect your own front you may
have to fire from some other battalion frontage right
or left.   In operating a very advanced Sniping Post,
where trenches are, say, 400 or 500 yards or more
apart, care should be taken not to walk enough in
one place to make a path that will be found by the
enemy patrols.   The result of this might be the
mining of your post by the enemy, or in any case it

would be the means of locating your Sniping Post.
If the post is entirely underground, it would be wise
to occupy another place close by. Have enough men
to capture or drive off enemy patrols, and keep them
from discovering your Sniping Post. In this connection one must bear in mind that the enemy send
out large patrols. It would be a great advantage in
such an advanced post to have a telephone, as it
would be unlikely that any other way of communication would be possible in daytime. We have ourselves occupied such posts and keenly felt the need
of a 'phone, mostly for the benefit of our artillery,
and also the O.C. Snipers, or something you
want the Rovers to look up, or decoys that you
might want displayed at a certain point. When
the trenches are far apart the enemy expose themselves a great deal more than when the opposite is
the case. Hence the great advantage of being so
close at hand, where you can shoot quickly and accurately. The forward slope of a hill is the best place
for a Sniping Post. If hill is narrow, tunnel through
from the rear; if not, dig down from the top and
tunnel out to the front. If you are not under some
trees or bushes, you must properly conceal the opening to correspond with the natural features; in some
cases it may be necessary to drain seepage into the
corner of the dugout and have a hand-pump, with a
rubber-canvas hose, to take the water some little
distance away. The hose must, of course, be concealed. If there is any rise in the ground at all such
a post can be made quite comfortable. In all these
kinds of dugouts you dig as near to the surface as
possible when you are tunnelling out for your loophole, and put two steel plates, one for each occupant,
tilting them inwards at the top, and support them so
that the slope of plate will be parallel to the slope of
the ground, and thereby get a wider angle of fire.
You dig out to the surface only the width and length

of the two plates, then widen out from there back, so that you can move your body and shoot at a wide angle. You must always locate the place you want your loophole from the front. You do this by going out at night and pushing a stick inwards. Mark the number of inches on it, and when you find it from the inside, while digging, you know exactly how far to the surface. If you don't do this, you might land right on a tuft of grass that you need to conceal your loophole. Also have the shelf that you are lying on considerably lower at your feet for comfort. Behind this point you dig down far enough to stand upright with ease. You can make yourself quite comfortable. The earth roof must be well timbered, to stand up well, as you might be there for a long time. If the water is not too close to the surface you may make your Sniping positions inside your dugout, to stand up to shoot, as when you shoot through a loophole you can get the different angles quicker when on your feet than when lying down. You can also tunnel into a patch of weeds from a disused trench, and river and creek bank. From a forward slope, covered with weeds, small brushes, etc., you can often have an open top post. If so you should have dug in the side a space that will shelter one at a time to lay down. It must be borne in mind that except in a few favourable circumstances all these differently located dugouts, with loopholes to shoot from, must be constructed at night. Only when you put such a dugout in your parapet or parados can you work at it in the daytime. A post in the parapet should be provided with a double loophole plate, the outer one being stationary, the inner one, being about 2 feet apart, should have slides in grooves, so as it will move with the rifle at different angles. Shooting straight out of one plate would not be much protection, but at any angle it would be next to impossible for the enemy to put a bullet through both loopholes.

Some of the old loopholes should be left, and the sentry go around and darken them up, so that the enemy will shoot at them. In all the trenches the parados should be higher than the parapet; this does away with the silhouette when anyone looks over, and it prevents the blowing back of shells. When much tunnelling and heavy construction is required in connection with this work, the O.C. Snipers should make requisition for assistance from the Tunnel and Pioneer Units in the vicinity.

If a well-constructed Sniping Post is being abandoned for some reason or other, it should be always blown up or otherwise destroyed, so that the enemy may not find out anything about our methods. A Sniping Post must be occupied all day in cases where you cannot enter or leave them without being seen. They must be occupied before daybreak and vacated after dark, when the listening patrol or guard, in the case of advanced posts, take cover. At dusk and dawn, when it is raining, and when a fog suddenly clears away, are most likely times for you to get a good shot at someone.

There should be two Sniping Posts on each company front, located to the best advantage 50 to 100 yards one way or the other. It does not matter, so that your own battalion front is your direct front; then each post watches the whole of the next company front on each side, so each company watches three company fronts; that means that twelve Snipers are watching every inch of ground at many different angles.

You will often come across local conditions where all the twelve men cannot observe the whole of the three companies' front, but you will often get a chance to shoot someone in the next company's front better than they have themselves, or even in the frontage of some other battalion. Besides these

twelve Snipers in organized Sniping Posts, there are
the Rovers and support company Snipers, who are
always on the alert. You must have the exact range
all along the enemy's parapet within your area, and
also have range of any prominent point in rear of
enemy's trenches if possible. As you will generally
have time to change the elevation of your rifle or
telescope sights, you should have your sights
adjusted for the average range, and for any other
range aim up or down accordingly; but if you can
adjust your sight very quickly, it is better to do so.
You make two range cards—one for each loophole.
The object of your setting ray must be the most
prominent point in the enemy's parapet; then you
can pick out other prominent objects all along the
enemy's parapet, not over ten in your sector, for if
you have more than that it will be hard to remember.
Now you number them off from left to right, including the setting ray point. You explain to the man
that relieves you that the setting ray point is so-and-
so. Of course, you draw rays on your range card
to every point along the enemy's parapet. Do not
draw rays to any point that you might be able to see
in the rear of the enemy's trenches. By using these
definite points and the clock method you can call
one another's attention to any given point in your
sector. If you want to call attention to an object on
the enemy's parapet, say between 4 and 5, if nearest
to point 5, you simply say point 5·9 ; if nearest to
point 4, you simply say point 4·3, meaning 3 or 9
o'clock.

The lower half of the clock face will be rarely used,
and upper half only when you see the ground or
objects in the rear of enemy's trenches. Then you
call out 10, 11¾, 12, 2, or 4 o'clock, as the occasion
demands, but 3 and 9 will be the figures mostly used.
With a little practice you will be surprised how
quickly you will be able to communicate locations.

Now, your range card must be of cardboard or very
thin wood, and painted the colour of the surroundings. You must, of course, have it small enough to
be able to place it under your loophole, but be careful
not to push it too near the surface, so that the enemy
will notice it. Never use white paper for range
cards. Officer Commanding Snipers must have a
range card for each Sniping Post for reference when
he reads your daily reports. Of course, you mark
the range on each ray. Any point in the rear of
the enemy's trenches you wish to call attention to
you write on the back of the range card, 5, 10, or 11
o'clock, 4 or 2 o'clock, as the case may be, and give the
range, also a description of the particular point you
wish to call attention to. If there is not enough
room on the back of range card, get an additional
card. You can write on both sides of this if necessary. These cards must always remain where they
belong; it does not matter who takes over the
trenches. Precautions must be taken that they do
not fall into the hands of the enemy. We have already
mentioned elsewhere how Snipers should be relieved,
both in their own unit and when a new battalion
takes over the post. The main point with a Sniper
is to be able to take instant and effective action when
in the discharge of his duties. For close observation from the trenches heat a steel plate, beat into
the shape of a sandbag, cover it with an empty
sandbag, or paint to suit. Place it in parapet, and if
done well it cannot be told from the regular sandbags. A small loophole 1 × 2 inches may also be
made to shoot through, by covering the outer edge
with two or three layers of sacking, with very ragged
edges around the hole. Of course, in a case of this
kind a place must be built around the hole to prevent
the silhouette effect, and the greatest care must be
taken in regard to your rifle. You always use this
precaution when you are shooting from concealed

posts in the trenches or parados. If enemy's trenches
are too close, the following will be effective. If you
have not already done so, pile up sandbags not less
than three deep on the outer face of trench.

When sandbags are settled into shape, you dig
through from the inside through the sandbags,
through the centre of the outer sandbag about 6 × 6
or 4 × 4 inches, so that you only have the single sacking left on the outside. Now you can see right
through the single sacking. You cannot be discovered from the front even at 10 yards, as the sack
will keep its shape, having been filled and settled
before. Sods or damp, stiff clay should be used for
this particular sack. If you can see through the
sacking you can aim through it. The bullet will
find its way through, and for a very short range this
method cannot be beaten.

PRECAUTION.—Keep your muzzle 4 feet back, so
that your discharge will not burst your single sacking. When fired through several times replace that
sack with another one, but be careful that you get
one of the same shade. This must be done at night.
It may be better to build a new post a few feet to
one side, and you will have no trouble with different
coloured sacking. If unarmed men approach don't
shoot, but keep them covered; don't expose yourself—take them prisoners if you can. If they are
voluntary prisoners, the Intelligence Officers will
want to see them as soon as possible. In this connection you must be very careful that it is not a trick
the enemy are trying to play on you, as they are
noted for this kind of game.

If any of the enemy come out to surrender in the
daytime in plain view of their own trenches, you may
be sure that they are trying to play a trick on you,
as their own men would shoot them down as deserters
unless this particular part of the line was unoccupied
by others. It is a common trick for them to call out

for you to come and take them. Don't go out. Let
them come in, and on any suspicious move shoot
them. If you went over they would drop down, and
their own men would shoot over their heads, and you
would be in a hot corner; also search àll prisoners, in
particular those who have volunteered to surrender,
for concealed arms. When you are stalking or
changing positions creep on your stomach, not
usually on hands and knees, unless by doing so you
are entirely out of sight. In a great many of these
cases, if you lay perfectly still, no one can see you.
If for some reason you have to move forward, and
cannot creep or crawl without being seen, do it in
short, quick spurts. Keep your body as near to the
ground as possible when lying down. Always choose
the best cover while laying down between spurts.
When you creep, keep your rifle in front of you.
When creeping on your stomach, don't move your
rifle and yourself at the same time. Put safety-catch
on rifle, and don't forget that it is on, and don't get
your rifle-muzzle full of dirt.

If, when you are constructing a Sniping Post,
your work is discovered, abandon it, but set a contact
mine, so that they will be sorry for their discovery.
Of course, this only applies to advanced posts. If
you can locate the enemy's advanced Sniping Post,
creep up in the night and capture guard quietly,
take possession, gather up any of the enemy patrols
that night who visit the post mine, and abandon
before daylight (contact mine). It would rarely be
practicable to occupy enemy's Sniping Post. If
such a thing were possible it would be only good for
one day, as they would in all cases find it out before
the second night. But if plans were carefully laid
and carried out they might lose a good many men
over one discovered advanced post. Take precautions
that they don't play a trick like this on you. And
Mining or Sniping Posts, referred to in these notes

in connection with your work, will be done by the
Engineers, at the request of your O.C. Snipers. The
only thing you must know in this connection is the
length to cut your fuse to suit your particular
purpose.

DECOYS AND THEIR USE.

We wish to impress on you that there is nothing
in which you are so liable to go too far in, or overdo,
as in the construction, and especially in manipu-
lating, decoys. Don't overdo it, whatever you do.
You can always go a little farther along the same
line if you find it necessary, but if you overdo it all
your work is lost, not only for you, but perhaps all
along the line. There are the most likely and the
most unlikely positions to place these decoys.

Get hold of some old clothing and rifles that are
beyond repair. You can easily make a figure to
represent a man by using a uniform stuffed with hay
or straw. Put heavy wire or wood inside to make it
rigid. Head and face can be made out of factory
cotton, stuffed with hay or straw. You make nose
and the rest of the body by making the material to
suit. Paint the eyes, make ears, and sew them on
hair; and beard, if necessary, can be made of horse-
hair or cow-hair of suitable colour and stuck on with
paint or glue.

Hair may also be made with unspun flax. Most
perfect heads can be cast in plaster, head and all
painted to suit, but they are very fragile. The closer
to the enemy's lines you are, the more perfect-made
decoys are required. You must make decoys to
represent English, French, and American soldiers.
By exposing a French soldier when they think they
know the English are occupying a position confuses
the enemy, and makes him eager to find out things,
and perhaps expose himself in doing so. It is up to
you to make these things look interesting to them.

When you are operating close to their lines you must have your decoys well made and manipulated, as the enemy have powerful telescopes. You can often place a figure in a tree, having one string or wire on each side to move the figure slightly. Again the prospects are that the enemy will expose himself. You can also place figures in the grass or undergrowth in No Man's Land, and move them slightly by strings to attract his attention. When you expose figures over the parapet, you show only the head, and in some cases the shoulders, and be sure to have figure duck every time it is shot at, whether it is hit or not. A figure of the head of a man with dummy field-glasses, looking over a parapet, will nearly always draw their fire. Decoys are rarely of any use unless they are movable or operated by strings, sticks, or wires from some safe place. In operating a line of decoys it must be borne in mind that artillery, as well as machine-gun and rifle fire, may be used by the enemy, so operators must govern themselves accordingly. Don't be too close to your decoys unless you are well dug in. You can always creep out in the morning before daylight, and put a few tin cans close into his wire or trenches. Have a strong wire or string attached hid in the grass. By rattling the cans you can, perhaps, excite his curiosity and get a good shot at him, particularly if it is raining heavily, and the trenches are a good distance apart, and your Snipers are occupying an advanced post. You can often use a looking-glass to flash the light into his trench, and in this way arouse his curiosity, and when he looks over to see what is going on again you have got your chance. Always look out that the enemy does not play a trick like this on you. Anything that you want to look at do so from a concealed place. You can also under these circumstances have hand-grenades placed close to the enemy's lines and arrange to explode them by pulling a string. If your trenches are located beyond hand-grenade range, it will most certainly excite his curiosity, particularly at dusk or dawn, heavy rain or fog. In practising the above ruses where there are likely to be several Huns showing themselves at one time it will be well for the observer to be ready to shoot. Also in case of an attack they should both shoot, but in all other cases only one man shoots from a post. You can also in many cases make fake Sniping Posts outside the lines and mine them, and when enemy patrols come to investigate blow them up. Such fake posts should be open-top ones.

RIFLE BATTERIES, THEIR CONSTRUCTION AND USE.

Rifle batteries, or set guns, may consist of one or more rifles (over ten or twelve rifles are not practicable) in one battery. They must be put in a concealed place, usually in a trench, but not necessarily so. Some other place on higher ground in rear of trenches may be better: sometimes they may be located up in a tree and worked from the ground. It might be dangerous to go up in the tree and reload, and if a great advantage is to be gained by operating this battery from this particular tree, a steel-plate cover could be constructed up in the tree for the protection of the operator. All guns in such a battery must be set, and be fastened in a very rigid frame, and must have barrel and butt fastened with the butt against something solid to take the recoil, so that they can be fired repeatedly without the aim of the individual rifle being disturbed.

If ten or twelve rifles are fired at once you can quite understand the need of a stand to hold them securely in place. After you get batteries set and aimed, you fasten the pulling wires to the triggers, bringing the string straight back to secure a straight

pull and put them into a guide of some kind ; it may
he an iron staple driven into the butt-rest, or between
two nails or a notch in the butt-rest. You now take
all the wires to a central point, and a short distance
in the rear or below, and fasten them to a ring or
piece of wood, and get them all adjusted with exactly
the same tension on the triggers, so that when you
pull the ring or wooden handle, all the rifles discharge simultaneously—that is, if you want the whole
battery to fire at once. If not, you can just pull the
individual wires to discharge whatever rifle you want,
as in a large battery all the rifles may not aim at the
same place, or for some reason or other you don't want
to fire more than one or two shots. If a battery aims
at several different places or objects, each section
should be operated from a separate ring or handle.
In constructing you must be very careful not to
make any noise, or you may give your position away,
and the battery would be rendered useless. Hay-
wire in particular will be found very useful for all
this work, except for pulling the trigger, and for
this you will find the small, insulated field telephone-
wire the best. These guns will be set to cover points
where you know the enemy will be operating at
night, to cover roads in rear or cross-roads where he
brings up men or supplies. You can also cut his
wire-entanglements in spots, or the artillery might
have done so. If you do it yourself it must be done
just before daylight, so they will not have time to
discover it and repair until the next night, and then
you would have a rifle battery laid to cover the place
the moment they start to work. If you, from your
observation post, know that the enemy is going to
repair a certain part of the trench the next night
(our artillery might have knocked its parapet down
in places), it will be a good idea to get a battery of
rifles to cover this spot, and when he starts to work
let him have it. If the trenches are very close

together you can perhaps observe for yourself when to fire. If too far away, a listening post should be located far enough in advance of your own lines to hear and see what is going on, and signal you when to fire your battery or any part thereof.

ALL RIFLES IN BATTERIES SHOULD BE NUMBERED.

Signalling of that kind is best done by pulling a wire one, two, or more pulls, as per arrangements between the operators. Rifles in batteries are laid in the daytime by the Snipers, but operated at night by the sentries or special men (not Snipers) told off for the work. These rifle batteries are not to be fired in the daytime unless under special circumstances. Whenever the battery or part thereof is fired, operators should at once reload, as he may be called upon to fire again at once. In loading, the operator must bear in mind that sound travels far at night, and work the bolt carefully. He must take care that his discharge has not brought on a regular fusilade, making it extremely dangerous to load for the time being; but chances are that if his battery is well concealed the enemy's fire will be directed elsewhere. Rifle batteries should always occupy a dominating or commanding position, high up, to get at the enemy's communication in his rear. Many times a rifle battery for night-firing can be constructed in a place where a Sniper would find it impossible to fire from during the daytime without being seen or heard. A single tall tree, for instance, where you could not shoot from, but by being careful you can work there in the daytime, laying your battery. In a case of this kind you would likely have to get your material and yourself up in the tree before daylight, and stay there all day. The more difficult these things are to do, the more effective they are likely to be. You can quite understand the importance of effective and efficient rifle batteries to be able to deliver fire at a given point on a dark night. It is very demoralizing to the nerve of the enemy. It all works in with the never-let-alone attitude. Strafe them night and day; give them no rest or peace, even for a minute; let them always be wondering what you are going to be up to next and where. Keep changing your tactics, and always have surprises on hand. Any rifle or periscope that the enemy exposes over his parapet should be instantly smashed.

MISCELLANEOUS.

The greatest precaution must be taken at night. It is necessary to train your men thoroughly in this work. Get them thoroughly trained and used to the dark.

People imagine thousands of things that do not exist. You hear many people say, " It's a cold, dark night; let us stay in !" Now, if it were just as cold by day, and they wanted to go out, they would do so. These fears of night are ridiculous in the extreme, and the only way to teach men is continuous training by night. You will find that the first few nights that they are out they will imagine everything, hedges as men, and after a few nights' training they see their own mistake, and they will gradually move about with as much confidence as they would by day.

Night, as we have said before, is the best, and perhaps the only, time that you can gain information from the enemy by patrol, so naturally the man accustomed to the dark will do the best work.

If he has hob-nails in his boots, etc., have him

G

originate some means whereby the sound will be deadened, such as pads, etc. Pads are very useful on the knees also, and very saving.

Each man on patrol work will want to take a pair of wire-cutters with him, in case at any time he may come across some obstacle that hinders his advancement. The time to train them into the proper way of cutting wire is now while you are at home. Wire is a very dangerous game to play with unless you are properly trained. You never know at what time your position will be given away, and perhaps a machine-gun aimed on the spot, if you tamper with and incorrectly cut the wire. You must train your men to hold the wire so that in cutting it the wire will not spring and cause an unnecessary amount of noise.

Accustom your men to the sound of men walking and running during day and night; also show them the distance between the heel of the fore-foot and the toe of the rear-foot when walking or running.

Similarly with horses walking, trotting, or galloping. Have them note the freshness of the mark, etc. When the infantry is out digging at night, take your men out and accustom their ears to the sound of the pick and shovel, with the wind against you, with you, and with no wind at all. This will be very useful when abroad, for once their ears are accustomed to the sound they will be able to pick it up again amidst the din. Accustom your hearing to sound of aircraft, find the direction from which it is coming, and the direction from which it is going. Practice in this will quicken you to pick up the direction of any aircraft abroad.

Those of you who have had experience on farms, or who have had shooting experience with prairie chicken or birds of any kind, know that they will rise on hearing the slightest noise. Birds' activity will aid you on many occasions to locate the enemy scouts.

Avoid trip-wires along enemy's front line; likely they are connected with flares, etc. Tape-lines, run out from your own trenches, will be useful for finding your way back. This is hardly necessary, though, with the Sniper Scout, as you should know your frontage in No Man's Land like a book.

A good way to train men to get them used to the outdoor life, Nature, and nights is to choose two camps concealed from each other by dead ground, perhaps three miles apart. Divide your men up, and man each of these camps and let them work against each other. Have them at all times under active service conditions. The camp itself will represent the battalion or brigade at the halt, and the Scouts will work on this assumption. Guards must be put out, and the protective screen must always be manned. Their work will consist of getting into each other's camp, drawing plans, positions of guards, reports on numbers, names of regiments, finding and manning positions that, through the telescope, each other's camps and each other's movements can always be noted. We did this with a brigade of Scout Snipers on Salisbury Plain, and the keenness and good work done was greatly appreciated.

Attached is a programme of training which we are now using. We think if your men are thoroughly trained in the subject specified, you might be quite sure that they will do the work abroad with the greatest of credit to the battalion or brigade. We do not pretend to know everything about Scout-Sniping, for it is one of the specialist branches, where there is something new to learn every day. The suggestions offered are not to be taken as hard and fast rules, but these notes we hope will be of advantage and helpful to those who are in the same position as we were on the day that war was declared.

CONCLUSION.

In conclusion, we wish to say that these notes do not by any means cover all the ways and means of a Sniper Scout, or organization of same operated at the front, but will serve as a foundation to start from, and the intelligent Sniper Scout on active service, from time to time, will be able to add a great many useful ideas, as he is confronted with the various conditions in the discharge of his duties. If this system and organization that we advocate in these notes were started in full swing all along the line to-day, you will be surprised on looking over the diaries and daily reports from Sniping Posts at the end of the week and see how many new and useful ideas have crept up in such a short time.

The more one goes in for this work the more interesting it is, and the more we realize of what utmost importance this branch of the Service really is. Entirely different from what it may appear at first glance, it is an extremely deep game, and should be played to the utmost limit. If entered into on these lines, a great many lives and much ammunition and other war material would be saved by the end of the war that would otherwise be lost. Our men at the Front are certainly worth saving. We lose considerable men in the ordinary course of events, without having them killed by enemy Snipers, and we have lost too many good fellows that way in the past.

We have lots of big-game hunters and Marksmen in our Army to draw from for this work, who, with a little special training along these lines and a proper organization, can make enemy Sniping impossible and life in their front line not worth living. Our Army as a whole can easily supply 5 per cent. of its total who can be trained as effective Sniper Scouts. Now, the organization which we advocate is about 4 per cent. We think that every Marksman and first-class shot should be trained in Sniping and Scouting, so as to have lots of men to draw from for this important work, and after completion of their training grade them, and employ them according to their individual ability.

If a unit has enough first-class shots for its full code of Snipers, let the others work with their companies as usual. They will make excellent men to have along the firing line at any time. We cannot have too many of such trained men, even if they are not actually employed as Sniper Scouts for the time being. The enemy have a regular system and organization regarding this work. They have the Schutzen battalions, the members of which are drawn from all over the German Empire, and have been in training for years. It is up to us to have at least the same or better, as we have far better men to draw from. We further very strongly want to impress upon you that as a Scout-Sniper you are thrown on your own resources to a large extent, and away from your superiors' immediate supervision. You must be a man in possession of a very strong sense of honour, and must feel the responsibility and trust placed in you, and not neglect your duty at any time because you may think you have an opportunity to do so. Yours is an all-the-time job; a few moments' neglect of your duty may be fatal to yourself and others. The more trust your superiors place in you the more responsibility you accept. If you don't do your utmost, you are helping the enemy to the extent of your neglect.

Even in comic papers of to-day you notice new and original jokes. Stale jokes are of no use. So it is in this specialist branch. Your mind must be continually concentrated to invent something new, as stale and old-fashioned methods are useless, and perhaps fatal in modern warfare.

This war is not going to be won by ancient rules and regulations, but original and up-to-date methods, and the methods employed in this branch lays entirely with the adaptability and capability of the individual Scout-Sniper.

In the attached syllabus of training for Scout-Snipers you will notice that the first period each morning calls for physical drill. This is very important, as physical fitness is the dominating factor in the choosing of a man for this work. A half-hour each day in Semaphore will be very helpful and useful, for you never know at what time this may be of use to you.

On the reconnaissance march for observation, explain to the men before going out clearly what to look for, and why they are going, and the Officer or N.C.O. in charge should take notes, so that the comparison can be made upon return.

In the foregoing notes map-reading has not been fully explained, but just sufficient for this specialist to grasp a general idea. Time and space forbid further explanation, as a complete knowledge of same is not requested. In field sketching and Panoramic drawing better results will be obtained if the men practise on landscape targets before drawing the natural features.

When marching on points with compass by day choose some area if possible where there is dead ground between your starting-point and objective. At night it does not matter.

As far as machine guns go, a Scout Sniper wants to know how to use and put out of action both Allied and enemy guns.

In practising the use of cover, the men want to be shown at different ranges the difference of men in khaki clothes and men dressed to assimilate the natural features. Show them how easy it is to see a man when his skin shows and how it is when the skin is coloured.

The lecture on Bombing is to train a man in the use of the Mills grenade, two of which are carried by every Scout-Sniper as a last resource.

You will want the Sergeant-Armourer of your battalion to lecture your men on the parts of the rifle and the effect of oil on certain parts; also have the Musketry Instructor lecture on zeroing, wind allowance, rapid aiming, cleaning arms, and care of arms in relation to accuracy, etc.

If you cannot arrange for loopholes to be fired from on the ranges, construct miniature posts and use ·22 ammunition, just to show them the means by which these practices are carried out. Too much practice with the ·22 ammunition is not advisable, for it might put the accurate shooter out with the ·303. The care and use of telescopic and magnifying sights must be thoroughly explained.

Gas, and the means of protection against same, must be practised. This is very important, for when a Sniper is in an advanced post he will be the first to feel the effects of the same; so you will have to practise quickness in putting on helmet, etc.

Aeroplane photographs will be studied, so that each Sniper will be able to see for himself, and read the same, the lay-out of the enemy's positions, and be taught just what to look for.

With regard to the shooting tests:—

    Practices I, II, III, IV, and V are to test the accuracy of the individual man and the accuracy of the rifle.

    ,,   VI and XV to practise quickness in shooting.

    ,,   VII, VIII, and XI to train eyesight to accurate shooting of small objects and indistinct objects.

Practices XII, XIII, and XIV to train a man
to judge distance, that he must aim
at in front of moving objects at
different ranges.

SHOOTING TESTS.

Practice.		Rounds.
I. GROUPING, 2nd Class Bull ..	100 yards	5
II. APPLICATION, 2nd Class Figure	100 ,,	5
III. Grouping, 2nd Class Bull ..	200 ,,	5
IV. APPLICATION, 2nd Class Figure	200 ,,	5
V. SILHOUETTE (Snap) (3 seconds)	200 ,,	5
VI. Firing at Loopholes	50 ,,	5
VII. Shooting and spotting con-cealed enemy (silhouette) ..	200 ,,	5
VIII. APPLICATION	300 ,,	5
IX. Firing at target behind cover..	200 ,,	5
X. Snapshooting (3 seconds) (sil-houette)	300 ,,	5
XI. Firing at target behind cover..	300 ,,	5
XII. Snapshooting at moving target	100 ,,	5
XIII. Snapshooting at moving target	200 ,,	5
XIV. Snapshooting at moving target	300 ,,	5
XV. Aiming position at known ob-ject (½ seconds exposure) ..	100 ,,	5

EXAMINATION : SCOUT-SNIPING.

(9.30–12 A.M.)

1. What are the personal qualifications of a good
Sniper ?

2. What are the three chief duties of a Scout-Sniper ?

3. How many men should man a Sniping Post, and
what is the work of each ?

4. How far is the flash of a rifle seen by day, with the
naked eye, with glasses ?

5. State five points that a Sniper must remember
when on night patrol.

6. Upon what would a Sniper report from an Observation Post ?

7. With whom must Sniping and Observation Posts be continually in touch with ?

8. When should a Sniper's Post be manned ? when quitted ?

9. How many men should you take for night patrols ? Why ?

10. Write a report to O.C. Snipers, 17th London Regiment, *re* enemy working on their wire.

11. Construct a scale of 3 inches to the mile, to measure yards.

12. Construct a scale of yards with R.F. $\dfrac{1}{1000}$

13. Into how many divisions or degrees is the compass divided ?

14. What is meant by Dip in a compass ?

15. Give three ways of finding True North.   Explain.

16. What is the variation of the compass here ?

17. Give two ways of setting a map.

18. Explain the following :—
        (*a*) Horizontal Equivalent.
        (*b*) Vertical Interval.

19. What does it denote when contours are close together ?

20. From Magnetic North, how do you find True North ?

21. Draw the following Conventional Signs :—
        (*a*) Embankment.
        (*b*) Cutting.
        (*c*) Tunnel.
        (*d*) Road over railroad.
        (*e*) Railroad over road.
        (*f*) Church with tower.

LOOPHOLES,

FIG 1

FIG 2

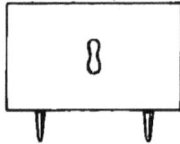 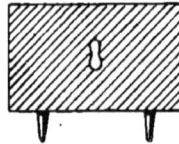

Take an ordinary steel plate. (*Fig.* 1.) Cover plate tightly with sacking or cloth, tightly sewed on. When sewed, cut hole for aperture, so that the shutters will work freely. (*Fig.* 2.)

FIG 3

FIG 4

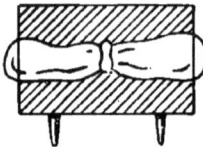 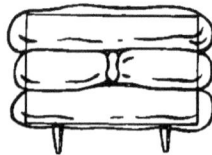

Take two sandbags, and fill them about half-full of rags or old torn sandbags, being particular to note that the corners are filled tightly. Having filled these sandbags half-full, turn down the choke ends and sew them up securely. Then sew one on each side of aperture as in Fig. 3, to correspond as near as possible with headers in solid parapet. (*Fig.* 3.)

Take two more sandbags for stretchers, and fill them as tightly as possible with old sacks or rags ; fill them to correspond as near as possible with the stretchers in permanent parapet. Then sew these stretchers securely to plate. (*Fig.* 4.)

FIG 5

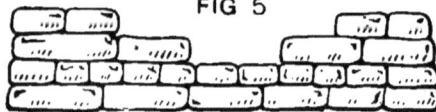

FIG. 5.—PARAPET PREPARED TO RECEIVE PLATE.

FIG 6

FIG. 6.—PLATE IN POSITION.

To prepare this plate successfully requires a certain amount of practice, particularly in filling the bags and sewing them up. (*Fig.* 6.)

NO. 2 CONCEALED PLATE ("FITZGERALD.")
(*Can be used in uneven or broken parapet.*)

FIG. 1

FIG. 1.—STEEL PLATE WITH SACKING SEWN TIGHTLY OVER IT, AND A HOLE CUT TO ENABLE SHUTTER TO WORK FREELY.

FIG. 2   FIG. 3

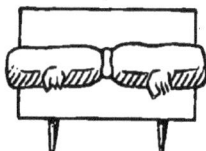 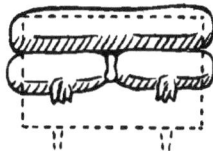

Fill up choke end of two bags about 10 inches in depth, or more if necessary. Fill fairly tightly, turn down, and sew up the ends, and sew these two dummy chokes to the plate. It is sometimes necessary to sew on three chokes in order to cover the plate completely. (*Fig.* 2.)

Fill and sew false stretcher to plate, being always careful to see that all parts of the plate are covered from front view. (*Fig.* 3.)

NOTE.—To obtain the best concealment with this plate, the dummy stretcher on the bottom of the plate should be dispensed with, and the plates placed low enough in the parapet to allow the false chokes to remain on the ground-level, as in Fig. 4.

92

FIG. 4.—SHOWS PLATE IN POSITION IN PARAPET
The steel lugs are driven into a filled sandbag for support.

FIG. 4

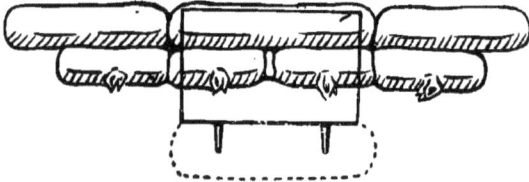

FIG. 4 A

For better protection, and to gain more room for the body, this
plate should have two steel wing plates ; this requires more
work. but is much better than sandbag protection. (*Fig. 4.*)

FIG 5.—WING PLATES IN POSITION.

FIG. 5

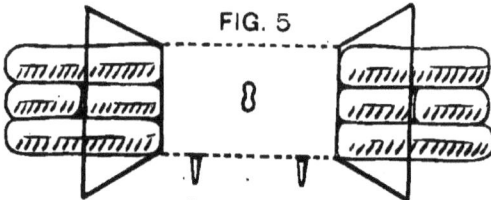

LOOPHOLE IN HEADER.

FIG. 1

FIG. 1.—STEEL PLATE WITH SACKING SEWN TIGHTLY OVER IT.

FIG. 3

FIG. 2

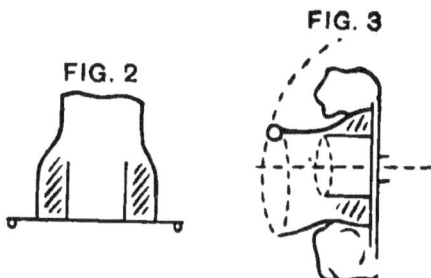

Place plate flat on the ground with front of plate uppermost. Then obtain piece of tin 10 inches and roll it a diameter of 6 inches, and fasten so that it will spring open. Place this tin over the aperture, and then get header sandbags and cut off the required length, and place over tin. Sew to sacking or plate. Then sew to shaded part (Fig. 2) between tin and bag, and pass stiff piece of wire through or around (threaded) neck of bag to keep it open. (*Fig.* 2.)

3.—CROSS SECTION, SHOWING SMALL WEIGHT FASTENED UNDER UPPER LIP OF SACK, AND LOOPHOLE OPEN IN READINESS TO FIRE.

FIG. 4

FIG. 4.—LOOPHOLE CLOSED.

FIG. 5

BOARD

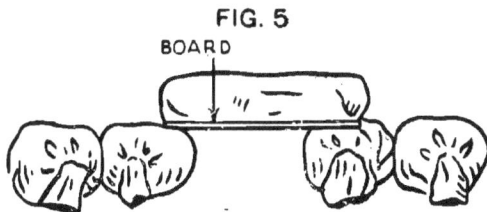

FIG. 5.—TO PREPARE PARAPET.

This loophole can be best concealed by being placed on ground-level; therefore leave space for false header, and place board over aperture, resting on headers as in Fig. 5. To support real stretcher, it is not necessary to have false stretcher. Plate in position with loophole open; wire passed over top of parapet. (*Fig.* 5.)

FIG. 6   WIRE

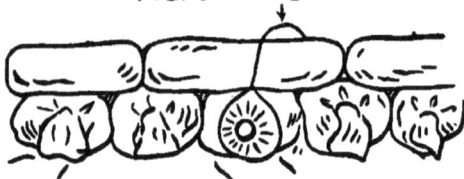

LOOPHOLE BETWEEN TWO ORDINARY HEADERS.

This loophole can be used in any parapet where bags are placed with the choke end outwards. This loophole is very difficult to pick up if properly manipulated. Steel plates can be used if required.

FIG. 1

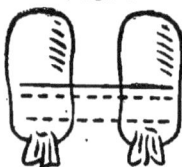

Place two header bags about 6 inches apart in the parapet. Then place a piece of board 1 inch by 6 inches across these bags, as in Fig. 1. Then take an empty sandbag and fold it to an oblong shape, about 6 inches wide, and sufficiently long to cover aperture effectively, as per dotted line in Fig. 1. You are now looking down on top of bags. (*Fig.* 1.)

FIG. 2

FIG. 3

STRETCHER

Now place genuine stretcher bag across aperture, and supported by 1-inch by 6-inch board, and also holding in place the dummy sacking, as in Fig. 2. (*Fig.* 2.)

Behind the sacking shutter is nailed a piece of wood about 1½ inches thick to keep shutter steady, and in front is nailed to the wood a false choke. To this false choke is attached a piece of signal wire and passed over the parapet. (*Fig.* 3.)

FIG. 4   OPEN

FIG. 5   CLOSED

MOUSE TRAP LOOPHOLE.

FIG. 1

NAIL HINGE

LID SHUT

FIG. 2

Mouse-trap loophole is very useful for concealment. Fig. 1 shows front of mouth of loophole as it will protrude flush with the parapet. (*Fig.* 1.)

Shows wooden frame of mouse-trap extending from steel plate to parapet. Lid of trap shut. Lid works on hinge. (*Fig.* 2.)

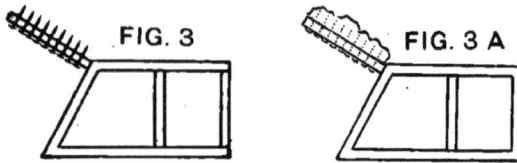

Mouse-trap with lid open, showing the nails driven outwards through the wood. On these nails can be placed sod, either with sod downwards or upwards, or with anything placed on to agree with the outward appearance of the parapet. This frame can be used, or an ordinary box can be cut to the correct angle. (*Fig. 3.*)

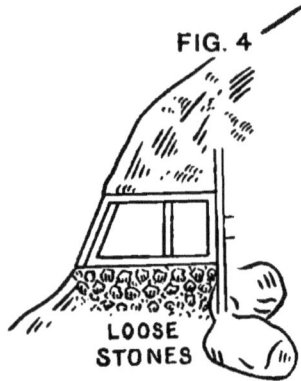

Shows the steel plate in position with the mouse-trap pressed close to the loophole in the plate, in readiness to receive the required disguise on the nail-points. (*Fig. 4.*)

LOOPHOLE WITH PLATE TURNED AROUND FOR TELESCOPIC SIGHT.

FIG. 1.—PLATE TURNED AROUND AND PLACED THE WIDTH OF STRETCHER (DIAMETER) FROM FRONT OF PARAPET.

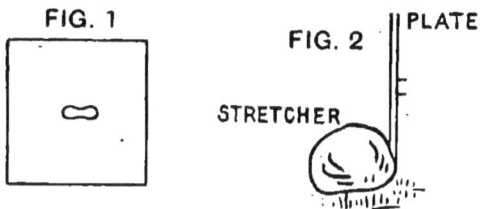

FIG. 2.—CROSS-SECTION OF PLATE IN POSITION.

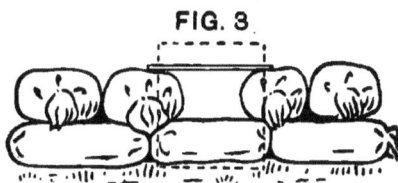

FIG. 3.—LOOPHOLE PARTIALLY COMPLETED WITH BOARD ACROSS HEADERS TO HOLD STRETCHER BAG AND FALSE CHOKE.

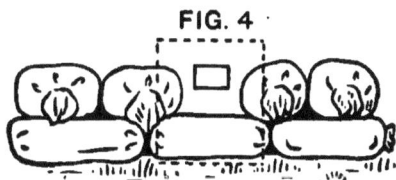

FIG. 4.—LOOPHOLE COMPLETED.

H

LOOPHOLES IN PARADOS.

FIG. 1.—SMALL WOODEN BOX PLACED IN STRETCHER SANDBAG IN PARADOS.

Difficult to observe, and to be used as a reserve loophole, to be fired from occasionally. Plate can be used here if necessary.

FIG. 2.—LOOKING DOWN UPON PARADOS.

Sew up a bag into three-cornered shape, as per Fig. 2, and place it slightly forward from flush to leave aperture for enfilade fire. Plate can be used if necessary. This loophole is being used with success in front-line parados. (*Fig.* 2.)

OBSERVATION BOX.—This box can be placed on top of parapet, let in about 1 foot or 18 inches, and gives good view, not easy to pick up ; several of them can be used on the parapet. Small pieces of tin painted can be used as a shutter. Forward aperture, about 4 inches by 6 inches ; rear aperture, about 14 inches. This box can also be used for observation in the parapet if made smaller.

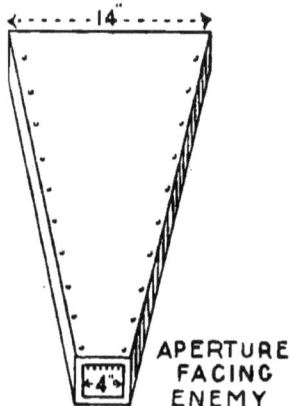

LOOPHOLE FOR OBSERVATION.

Take a new sandbag and cut along dotted line—one side only, leaving other intact. (*Fig.* 1.)

Turned around, the bag now looks like a shaving-case, with pocket at bottom or header end. This pocket is now filled with old rags or bags to represent a dummy header. When carefully filled, a piece of board of the same shape as the header is placed in behind the rags sufficiently deep to allow the edge of the pocket being pulled across and sewed to remaining side of sandbag. One side of the sandbag is left intact in order to hold the dummy header in position, and also to act as a hinge for opening and shutting. (*Fig.* 2.)

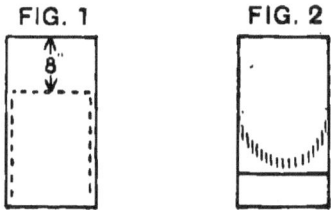

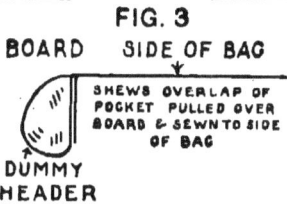

FIG. 1

FIG. 2

FIG. 3

BOARD   SIDE OF BAG

SHEWS OVERLAP OF
POCKET PULLED OVER
BOARD & SEWN TO SIDE
OF BAG

DUMMY
HEADER

FIG. 3.—SIDE VIEW OF DUMMY HEADER, AND REMAINING SIDE OF SANDBAG IN READINESS TO BE PLACED IN POSITION.

SIDE VIEW

FIG. 4

OPEN   CLOSED

FIG. 4.—DUMMY IN POSITION IN PARADOS, REPRESENTED BY SHADED BAG.

A piece of board is placed across sandbags 1 and 2, in order to support stretcher bag No. 3, and at the same time to hold dummy in position. (*Fig.* 4.)

H 2

BOX LOOPHOLE FOR EARTH PARAPET.

Fig. 1.—Ground Plan of Box, showing Position of Plate
and Field of Fire.

Box can be short or long, according to circumstances ; the shorter
the better. The front of the box should be cut at an angle,
in order to conform to the slope of the parapet. (*Fig.* 1.)

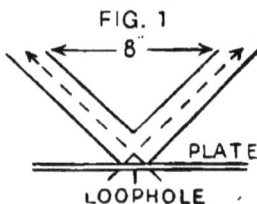

FIG. 1

PLATE

LOOPHOLE

Fig. 2.—Front View of Box and Plate in Readiness for
Parapet.

The dimensions of the box depend largely upon conditions of
the parapet and opportunity for concealment. If careful
concealment is necessary, the box aperture should not be
larger than 4 inches by 3 inches. These apertures should
be closed by means of a wooden door of the same size.
This door can be hinged either from side or top, and opened
by wire attachment. Concealment can be arranged in usual
manner by driving nails through door, and placing on these
nails anything which conforms to the background or general
colour of parapet. (*Fig.* 2).

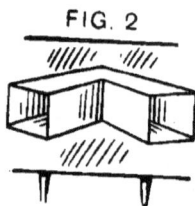

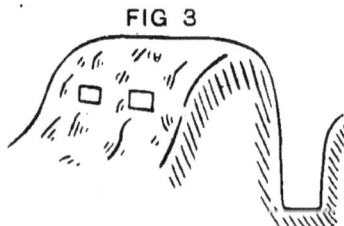

FIG. 2   FIG 3

Fig. 3.—Section of Earth Parapet showing the Loophole
in Position, but not yet Disguised.

Small sods grass downwards, and placed on the above-mentioned
nails, provide very good concealment. This loophole gives
a very much larger field of fire than the ordinary aperture.
and is safer.

SYLLABUS OF TRAINING FOR SNIPERS.

THURSDAY..
A.M. — Physical Drill. Semaphore. Duties of Scout. (a) Qualifications. (b) Kind of Men Wanted. (c) Day Work. (d) Night Work. (e) Observation Posts. (f) Firing Posts. (g) Night Patrols.
P.M. — Reconnaissance March for Observation.

FRIDAY ..
A.M. — Physical Drill. Semaphore. Intelligence. Elementary Map Reading. Field Sketching. Compass (Prismatic, Oil and Plain).
P.M. — Marching on Points. Finding one's Way by Map, Compass, Sun, etc.

SATURDAY ..
A.M. — Physical Drill. Semaphore Interior Economy.

MONDAY ..
A.M. — Physical Drill. Semaphore. Observation of Ground. Judging Distance. Visual Training. Use of Periscope, Hypo-scope, Telescope, and Field-Glasses.
P.M. — Construction of Loop-holes.

TUESDAY ..
A.M. — Physical Drill. Semaphore. Report Writing. Map Reading.
P.M. — Traversing.

WEDNESDAY
A.M. — Physical Drill. Semaphore. Map Reading (Advanced). Lecture, Night Scouting.
P.M. — Field Sketching.

SYLLABUS OF TRAINING FOR SNIPERS—(*Continued*).

	A.M.	P.M.
THURSDAY..	Physical Drill. Semaphore. Use of Ground and Cover. Selection of Likely Posts, with Sketches of Frontage.	Criticism of Posts.
FRIDAY ..	Physical Drill. Taking up Posts under Active Service Conditions by Day.	Digging in Posts by Day.
SATURDAY ..	Physical Drill. Lecture, Mills Hand Grenades. Interior Economy.	
MONDAY ..	Physical Drill. Semaphore. Post Digging.	Lecture, Parts of Rifle. Digging in Posts by Night.
TUESDAY ..	Physical Drill. Semaphore. Criticising Night Digging.	Marching on Points.
WEDNESDAY	Physical Drill. Semaphore. Aiming and Trigger-Pressing. Principle of Aiming and Sights. Wind Allowance. Rapid Aiming. Cleaning Arms. Care of Arms in Relation to Accuracy.	Outdoor Training with Telescopes and Field-Glasses. Making Reports on Given Frontage with Help of Range Card & Sketches.
THURSDAY..	Physical Drill. Semaphore. Zeroing. Miniature Range.	Fitting of Telescopic and Magnifying Sights.

SYLLABUS OF TRAINING FOR SNIPERS—(*Continued*).

	A.M.	P.M.
FRIDAY ..	Physical Drill. Semaphore. Handling of Rifles in Field. Visual Training from Posts in the Open.	Demonstration of Firing through and at Loopholes.
SATURDAY ..	A.M. Physical Drill. Lecture by Machine-Gun Officer on " How to Use and Put Out of Action Allied and enemy Guns."	
MONDAY ..	A.M. Physical Drill. Snapshooting behind Cover at Men appearing over Parapet. Spotting and Shooting Concealed Enemy.	P.M. Locating and Firing at Difficult Targets from Behind Cover. Snapshooting. Allowance for Movement.
TUESDAY ..	A.M. Physical Drill. Snapshooting at Moving Targets. Visual Training.	P.M. Rifle Batteries.
WEDNESDAY	A.M. Physical Drill. Lecture on Gas.	P.M. Recapitulation. Map Reading. Compass Sketching, etc.
THURSDAY..	A.M. Physical Drill. Examination in Scouting.	P M. Examination in Sniping.
FRIDAY ..	A.M. Physical Drill. Correcting Papers and Explaining Mistakes.	P.M. Lecture on Gas.

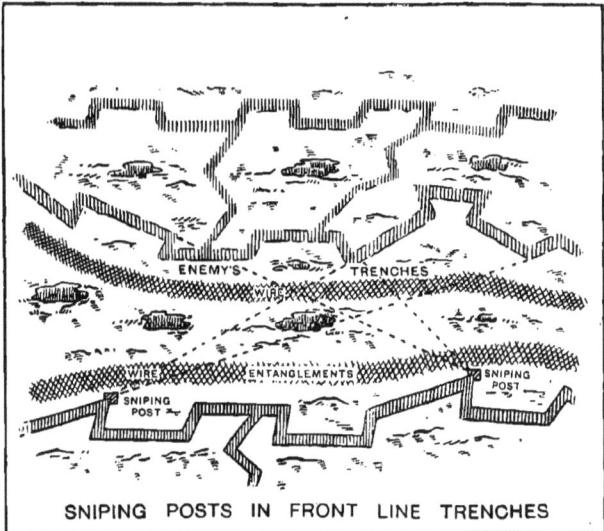

SNIPING POSTS IN FRONT LINE TRENCHES

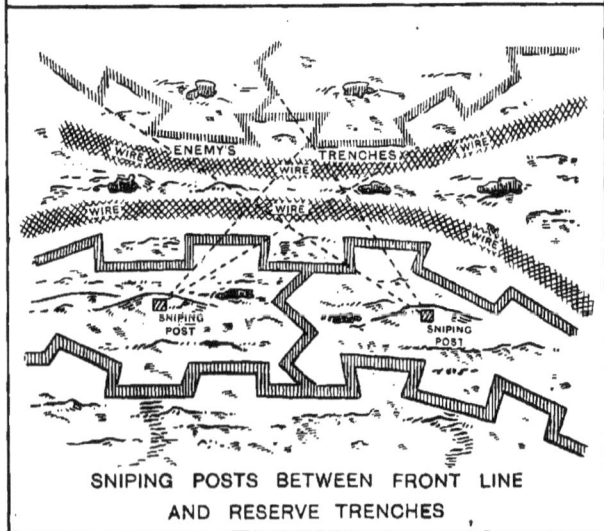

SNIPING POSTS BETWEEN FRONT LINE
AND RESERVE TRENCHES

Always keep Muzzle of Rifle well back from loophole
NEVER Shoot as shown

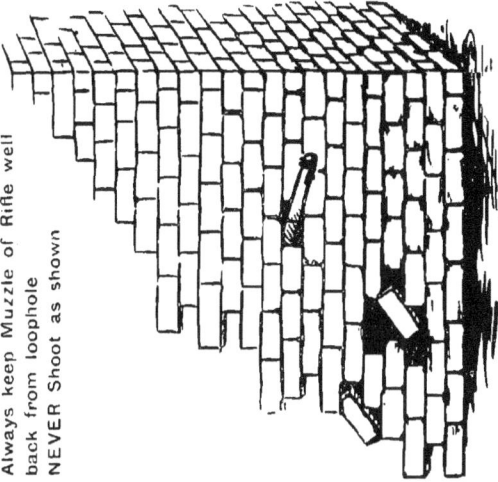

NEVER look over Rails as above, but dig down and shoot between the Ties or Sleepers Tunnel through Rail Road from opposite side

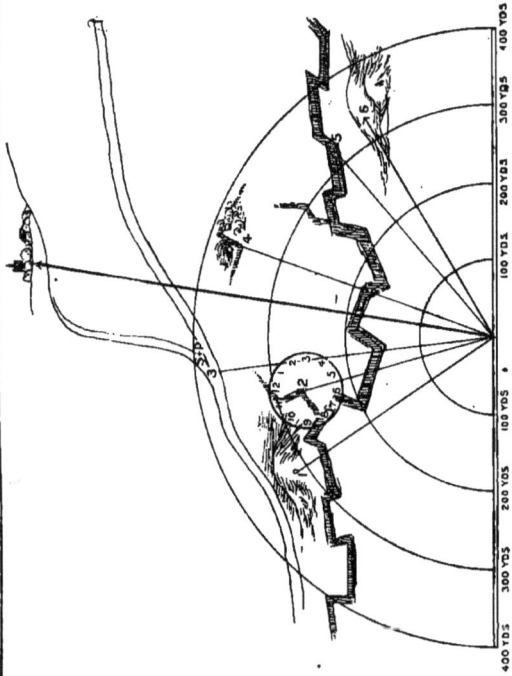

RANGE CARD.

With rays and clock method.

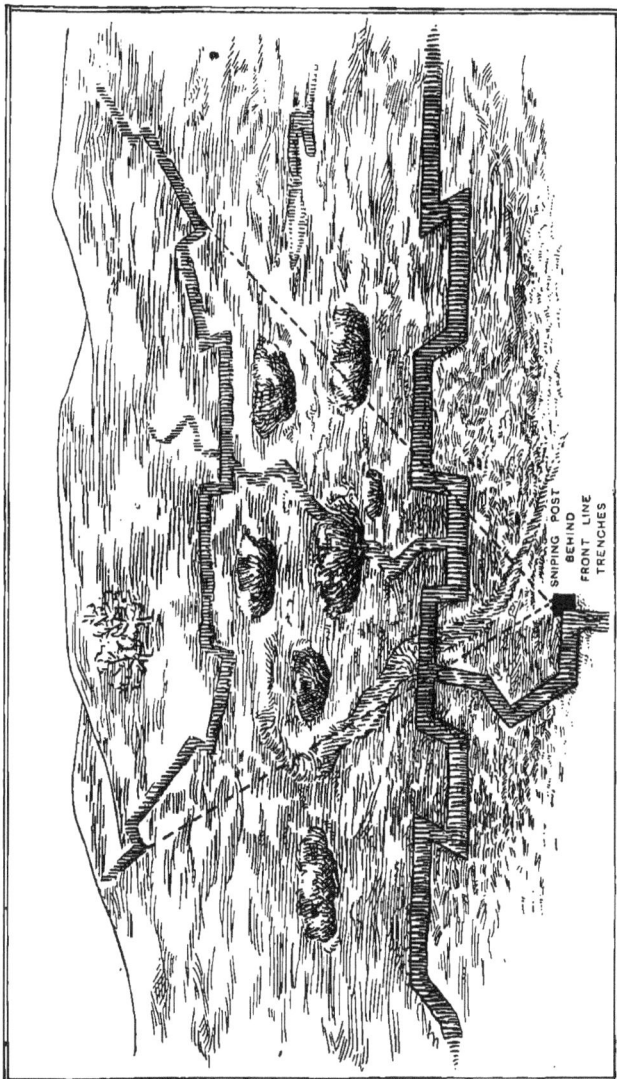

SNIPING POST BEHIND FRONT LINE TRENCHES

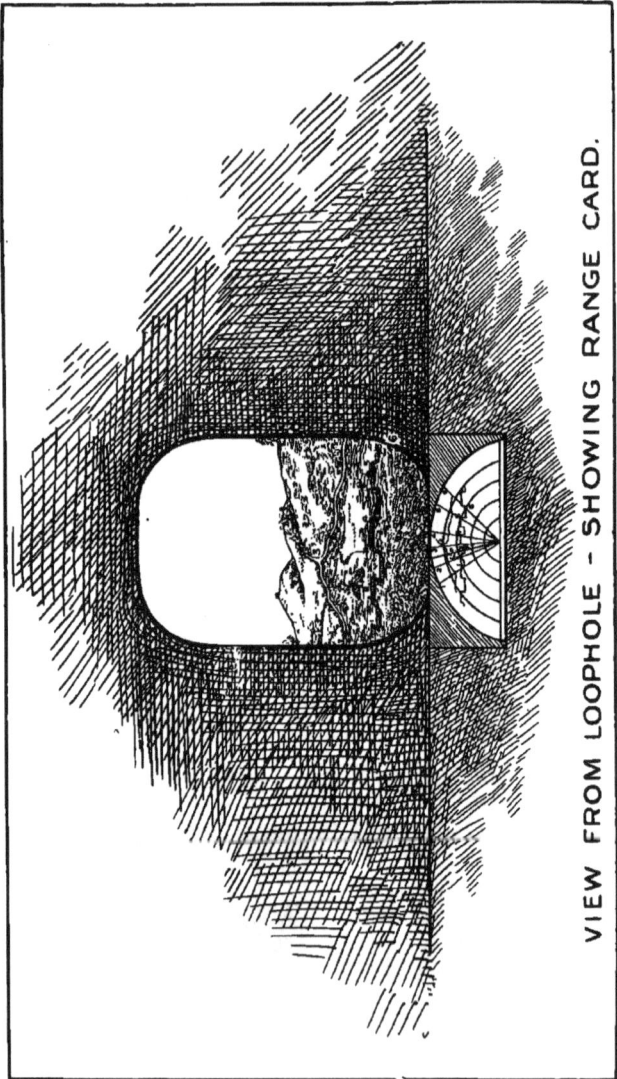

VIEW FROM LOOPHOLE - SHOWING RANGE CARD.

PLATE XI.

INTERIOR OF LYING SNIPING POST (REAR VIEW)

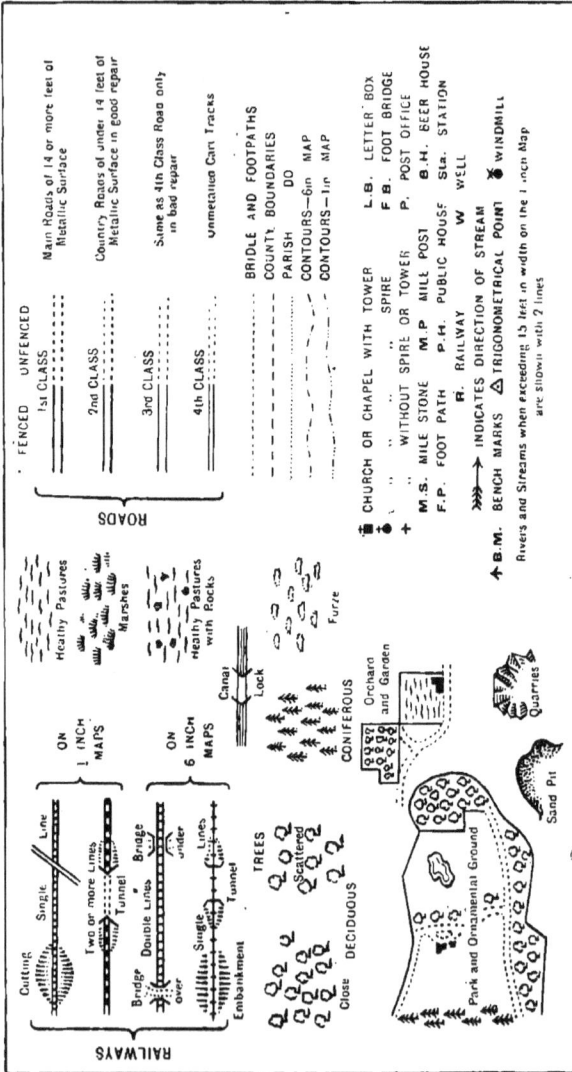

SYMBOLS USED ON THE 1 INCH AND 6 INCH ORDNANCE MAPS

Plate XIII.

THE WRONG WAY TO SHOOT THROUGH A WINDOW

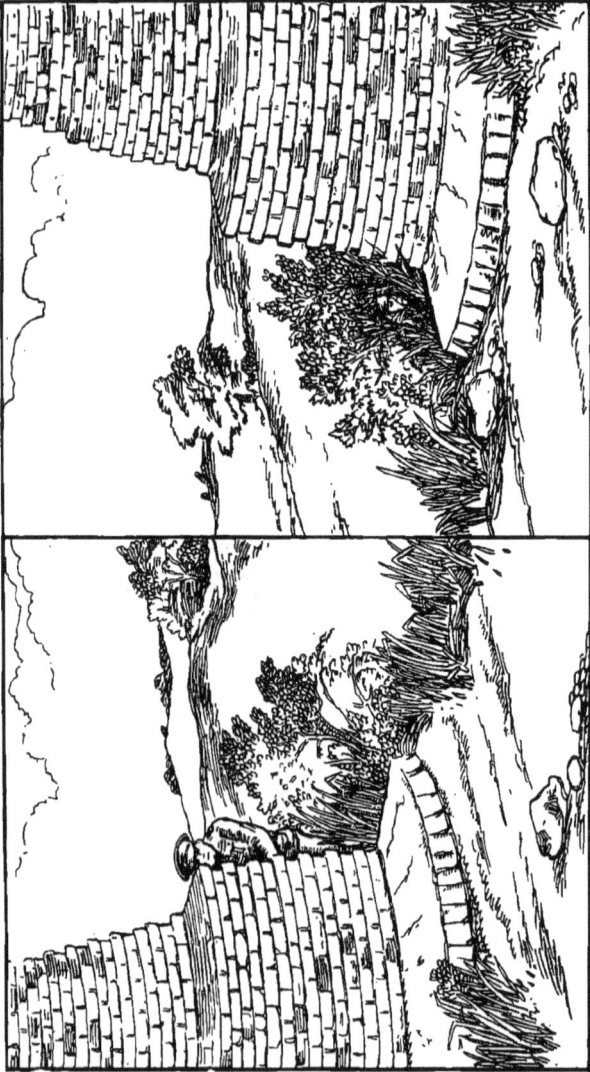

When out Scouting always lie down to look around a corner, taking advantage of all Natural Cover, and whenever possible look from your right or Firing side

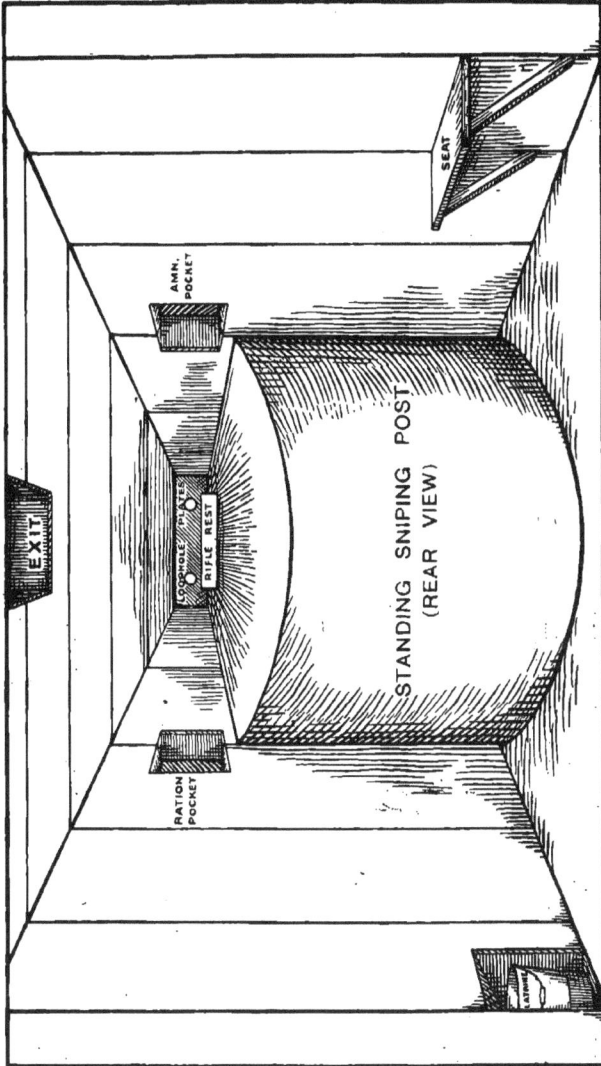

STANDING SNIPING POST
(REAR VIEW)

SEAT

AMN. POCKET

EXIT

LOOPHOLE PLATE

RIFLE REST

RATION POCKET

NOTE MUZZLE BACK FROM LOOP HOLE.

RIFLE REST

AMN. POCKET

EXIT

LATRINE

STANDING POST.

Sectional View of Lying Post.

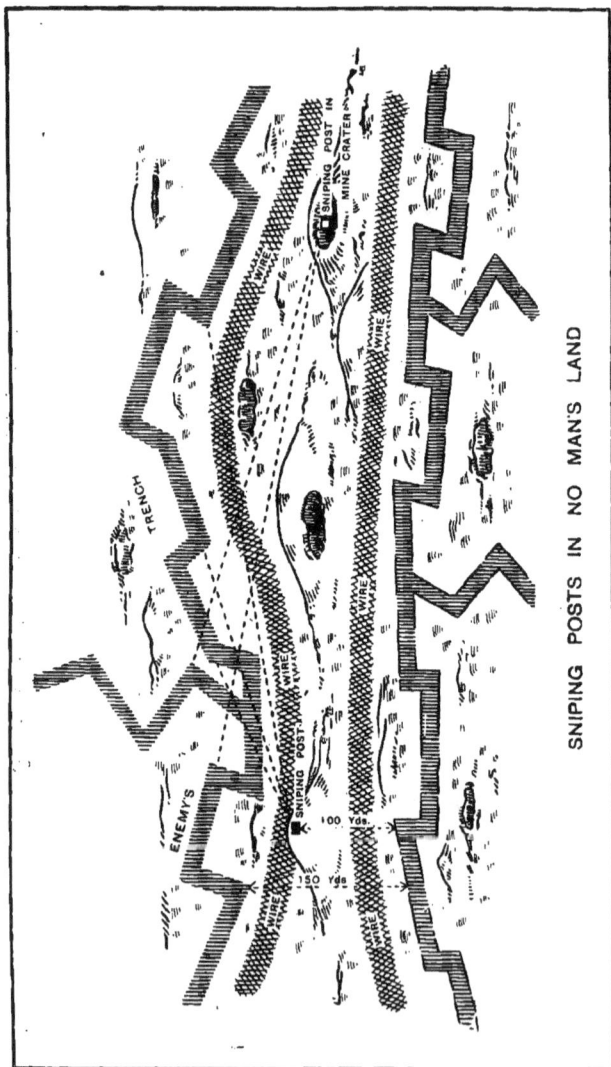

SNIPING POSTS IN NO MAN'S LAND

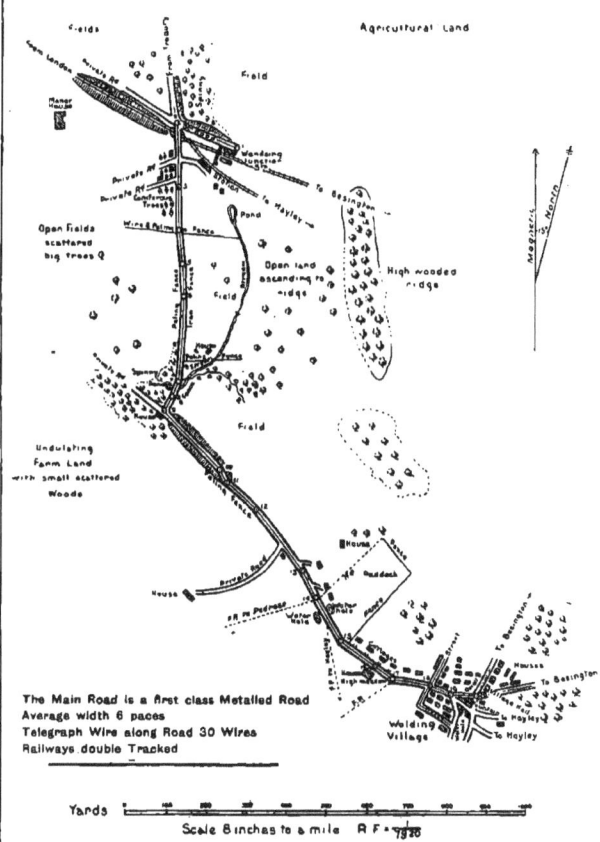

PLOT OF ANOTHER TRAVERSE

The Main Road is a first class Metalled Road
Average width 6 paces
Telegraph Wire along Road 30 Wires
Railways double Tracked

Yards

Scale 8 inches to a mile   R F = 1/7920

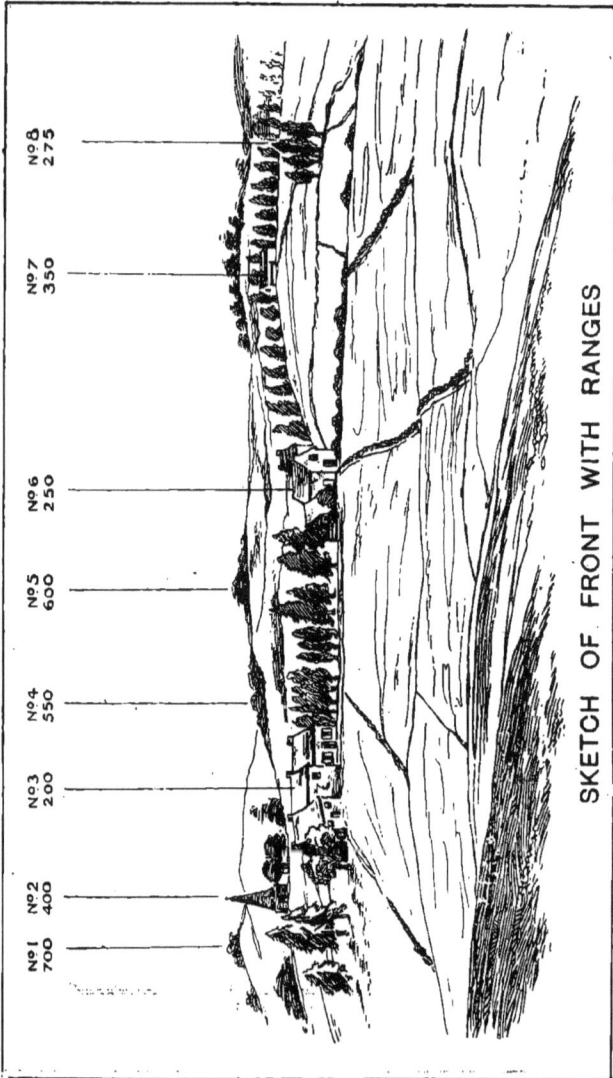

No I   No 2   No 3   No 4   No 5   No 6   No 7   No 8
700   400   200   550   600   250   350   275

SKETCH OF FRONT WITH RANGES

www.ingramcontent.com/pod-product-compliance
Lightning Source LLC
Chambersburg PA
CBHW071226090426
42736CB00014B/2987